**Windows 98**

Windows is a registered trademark of Microsoft Corporation.
All other trademarks quoted are the property of their respective editors.

All rights reserved. No part of this publication may be reproduced, stored in a retrieval system, or transmitted, in any form, or by any means, electronic, mechanical, photocopying, recording or otherwise, without the prior permission of the publishers.

Copyright - Editions ENI - November 1999
ISBN : 2-7460-0864-5
Original edition : 2-7460-0632-4

## ENI Publishing Ltd

500 Chiswick High Road
LONDON W4 5RG

Tel: 020 8956 2320
Fax: 020 8956 2321

e-mail: publishing@ediENI.com
http://www.editions-eni.com

## Editions ENI

BP 32125
44021 NANTES Cedex 1

Tel: 02.40.92.45.45
Fax: 02.40.92.45.46

e-mail: editions@ediENI.com
http://www.editions-eni.com

**Finding your Way** Collection directed by Corinne HERVO
Translated from the French by Adrienne TOMMY

# FOREWORD

The **Finding Your Way** collection is aimed at people with no previous experience in computing. It has been put together to give you clear and detailed explanations, using precise and simple terms. These explanations keep to the rule "one description, one illustration": each command is illustrated with a dialog box or a screen showing an example:

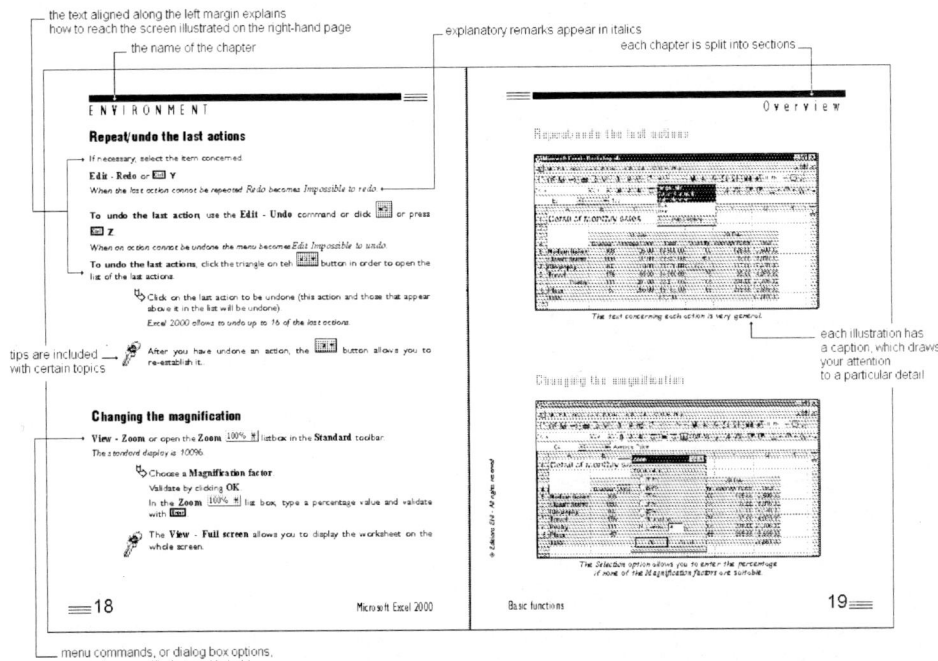

To give you as wide an introduction to the software as possible, all the methods of performing each task have been described. The following icons have been used to identify them: (menu method), (mouse method) and (keyboard method).

Every book in the **Finding Your Way** collection is organised in chapters, which are split into sections dealing with particular topics. The general layout of the book is presented in the **Table of contents**, which you will find on the following pages.

The book includes an appendix with a list of the shortcut keys available and an **Index**, for finding information quickly.

1

# Table of Contents

## OVERVIEW          Chapter 1

### ■ ENVIRONMENT

| | |
|---|---:|
| Starting Windows 98 | 8 |
| Looking at the Desktop | 10 |
| Using the Start menu | 12 |
| Switching off the computer | 14 |
| Starting/Leaving an application using the Start menu | 14 |
| Managing windows | 16 |
| Changing the size of a window | 16 |
| Managing more than one window | 18 |
| Closing a window | 18 |
| Managing application menus | 20 |
| Managing application menus | 20 |
| Working in dialog boxes | 22 |
| Getting help in a dialog box | 24 |
| Using the Windows help menu | 24 |
| Undoing your last action | 26 |
| Accessing drives without the Explorer | 26 |
| Accessing shared folders without the Explorer | 28 |

### ■ DOCUMENTS

| | |
|---|---:|
| Opening a document from an application | 30 |
| Opening a document from the Start menu | 32 |
| Creating a document from an application | 32 |
| Saving a new document | 34 |
| Saving an existing document | 34 |

## WORDPAD          Chapter 2

### ■ OVERVIEW

| | |
|---|---:|
| Choosing the items you need in the window | 38 |
| Moving the toolbar and Format bar | 38 |
| Moving the insertion point | 40 |
| Selecting text | 40 |

## ■ ENTERING/EDITING TEXT

| | |
|---|---|
| Entering/changing text | 42 |
| Inserting the date and time | 42 |
| Finding text | 44 |
| Transferring text without the clipboard | 44 |
| Replacing text | 46 |
| Copying/moving text using the clipboard | 46 |

## ■ FORMATTING TEXT

| | |
|---|---|
| Applying attributes to characters | 48 |
| Changing the font | 48 |
| Changing the font size | 50 |
| Colouring characters | 50 |
| Changing the character attributes font, size and colour | 52 |
| Changing the indents | 52 |
| Changing the indents | 54 |
| Changing the alignment of a text | 54 |
| Inserting a bullet at the beginning of a paragraph | 56 |
| Using tabs | 56 |
| Setting tabs | 58 |
| Managing tabs | 58 |

## ■ PRINTING

| | |
|---|---|
| Displaying a print preview | 60 |
| Changing print margins and orientation | 60 |
| Printing a document | 62 |
| Managing the print queue | 64 |

# PAINT                                    Chapter 3

## ■ OVERVIEW

| | |
|---|---|
| Looking at the Paint window | 68 |
| Moving the tool box or the colour box | 68 |
| Changing the size of the image area | 70 |
| Creating a drawing | 70 |

Windows 98

### ■ MAKING A DRAWING
Drawing a rectangle, a square, a circle or an ellipse  72
Drawing a straight line or a curve  74
Drawing polygons  76
Managing text  78

### ■ EDITING A DRAWING
Erasing a drawing  80
Moving a drawing  80
Selecting part of the image  82
Copying an image inside the image area  82
Copying part of an image into a new document  84
Copying the content of a document into the Paint window  84
Painting an area  86
Creating a custom colour  86
Managing colours  88
Wallpapering the Desktop  88
Zooming in on an image  90
Working in Zoom mode  90
Resizing an image  92
Resizing an image  92
Skewing an image  94
Rotating an image  94

## EXPLORER  Chapter 4

### ■ VIEWING DISK CONTENTS
Looking at the Explorer window  98
Managing views of the Explorer  100
Going into a drive/a folder  102
Setting out the list of documents  104
Sorting the list of documents  104

### ■ FOLDERS AND DOCUMENTS
Selecting documents  106
Deselecting documents  106
Searching for one or more documents by name  108
Searching for one or more documents by modification date  110
Creating a folder  110

Windows 98

| | |
|---|---|
| Copying folders or documents using the clipboard | 112 |
| Copying folders or documents 🖱 | 112 |
| Copying folders or documents onto a diskette | 114 |
| Renaming a folder or document | 114 |
| Moving a folder or documents using the clipboard | 116 |
| Moving a folder or documents 🖱 | 116 |
| Deleting a folder or documents | 118 |
| Opening an application from the Explorer | 118 |
| Managing folders/documents located in the Recycle Bin | 120 |
| Printing a document from the Explorer | 120 |
| Sharing a folder with network users | 122 |

## MULTIMEDIA — Chapter 5

### ■ CD PLAYER
| | |
|---|---|
| Listening to an audio CD | 126 |
| Naming and selecting tracks on an audio CD | 128 |
| Playing a multimedia file | 128 |

### ■ MEDIA PLAYER
| | |
|---|---|
| Copying part of a multimedia file | 130 |

### ■ SOUND RECORDER
| | |
|---|---|
| Playing a sound file (Sound Recorder) | 132 |
| Recording with a microphone | 134 |
| Modifying sound files | 136 |

## OLE/CONFIGURATION — Chapter 6

### ■ OBJECT LINKING AND EMBEDDING
| | |
|---|---|
| Inserting an existing document into another document | 140 |
| Inserting a new document into another document | 142 |
| Managing a link with an external object | 144 |
| Modifying an embedded object | 144 |
| Displaying an embedded object as an icon | 146 |

## ■ CONFIGURATION

| | |
|---|---|
| Clearing the Documents menu | 148 |
| Creating a shortcut on the Desktop | 148 |
| Presenting the Desktop | 150 |
| Modifying the control date and time | 152 |
| Managing the taskbar | 152 |
| Installing a printer | 154 |

## APPENDIX

| | |
|---|---|
| Shortcut keys | 157 |
| Index | 159 |

# Chapter 1

## OVERVIEW

- **ENVIRONMENT**     p.8
- **DOCUMENTS**     p.30

## OVERVIEW

## Starting Windows 98

*Windows 98 is an operating system with a graphical interface, created by the Microsoft corporation for PC type computers. If the DOS (the previous operating system) is still in place, you can access it from Windows 98.*

When you switch on your computer, Windows 98 is loaded automatically into the central memory. If your computer is part of a network, you may be asked to supply a password.
You may now see a **Welcome to Windows 98** dialog box.

> **To register** your copy of Windows 98, click the **Register Now** option.
> 
> **To connect to Internet** without delay, click the **Connect to the Internet** option.
> 
> **To explore Windows 98**, click the **Discover Windows 98** option.
> 
> **To setup a periodic maintenance programme** for Windows, click the **Maintain Your Computer** option.
> 
> **To avoid seeing the dialog box at every startup**, deactivate the **Show this screen each time Windows 98 starts** option.
> 
> **To close the dialog box**, click the ⊠ button.

# Environment

## Starting Windows 98

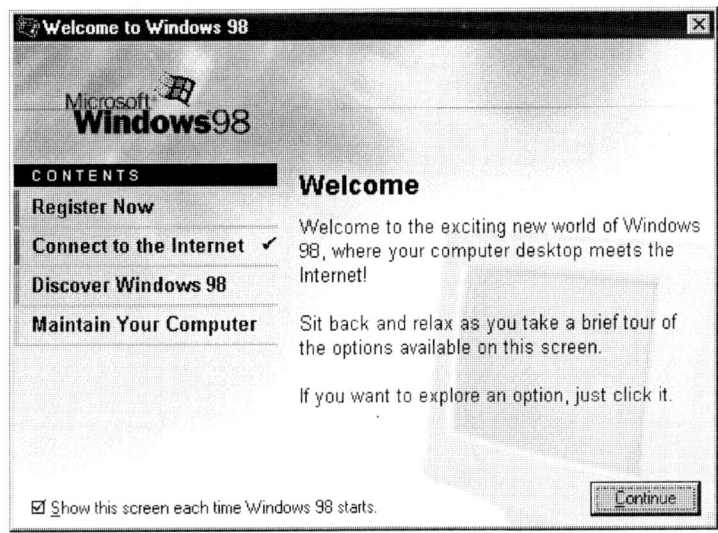

OVERVIEW

## Looking at the Desktop

After closing the **Welcome** dialog box, a workspace appears on the screen, called the **Desktop**. The presentation and contents of the Desktop can be customised, and so vary from one computer to the next.

☞ You should still find the following components:
- The **Taskbar** (a), an easy way into the tasks, or active applications, which appear on it as buttons.
- The **Start** button (b) which opens the Windows 98 Start menu.
- The **My Computer** icon (c) gives you quick access to the various drives of the PC, and to the **Printers** folders, the **Control Panel**, **Dial-Up Networking** and the **Scheduled Tasks**.
- The **Network Neighborhood** icon (d) appears if your computer is part of a network (Windows 98, Windows NT, Novell...).
- The **My Documents** folder (e) will store for you any documents (of any type) to which you require immediate access.
- The **Recycle Bin** (f) allows you to retrieve documents or folders deleted by mistake.
- The **Clock** (g) which shows you the time set on the computer.
- The **Quick Launch** bar (h) speeds up access to the Desktop, the channels, Internet Explorer and Outlook Express.
- The **Task Scheduler** (i) enables you to schedule applications installed on your computer to run automatically.
- The **Connect to the Internet** shortcut (j) starts the Internet Connection Wizard.
- The **Online Services** folder (k) allows you to sign on with an Internet Service Provider (the ISPs proposed in Windows 98 are AOL, CompuServe, AT&T, Prodigy and the Microsoft Network).
- The **My Briefcase** folder (l) stores files that you can access easily from another computer, at home or while travelling.
- The **Channel Bar** (m) contains pre-set shortcuts to a selection of Web sites. To close this bar, click the ☒ button in the top right corner.

*Other icons (objects) can also appear on the Desktop, such as shortcuts into various applications or documents.*

Environment

## Looking at the Desktop

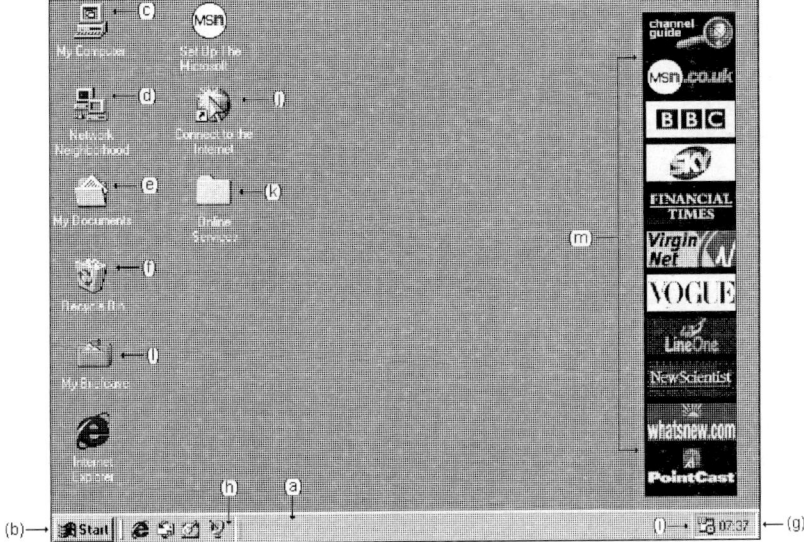

Double-click the clock (g) to open the dialog box which allows you to change the system time and date (cf. Modifying the system date).

Windows 98

OVERVIEW

## Using the Start menu

**To show the Windows 98 Start menu**, click the Start button or use `Ctrl` `Esc`.

**To open a submenu**, move the pointer onto the **Programs** option.

*The submenu opens automatically: notice that it too contains a set of submenus.*

☞ The Windows 98 start menu contains several items:
- The **Programs** menu groups together the applications installed under Windows 98 (there may be other applications on your disk which are not accessible from this menu).
- The **Accessories** menu contains the various accessories available in Windows 98 (the Calculator, Notepad, Paint, WordPad...).
- The **Favorites** menu gives you access to your favourite Web sites, if you are connected to the Internet.
- The **Documents** menu contains a list of the last 15 documents used to ensure quick access. You can erase the contents of this menu.
- The **Settings** menu allows you to reorganise your working environment (Desktop, printers, taskbar...). The first two options can also be reached via **My Computer**.
- The **Find** option helps you search for files (documents), folders or other computers in your network. The **On The Internet** option starts Internet Explorer so you can search on the Web.
- The **Help** option accesses the Windows 98 help.
- The **Run** option runs a program from the corresponding executable file.
- The **Log Off** option lets you disconnect and reconnect under another user name without having to restart your computer.
- The **Shut Down** option should be activated before switching off your computer.

**To close the Start menu**, click anywhere else on the Desktop or press `Esc` as many times as is necessary.

# Environment

## Using the Start menu

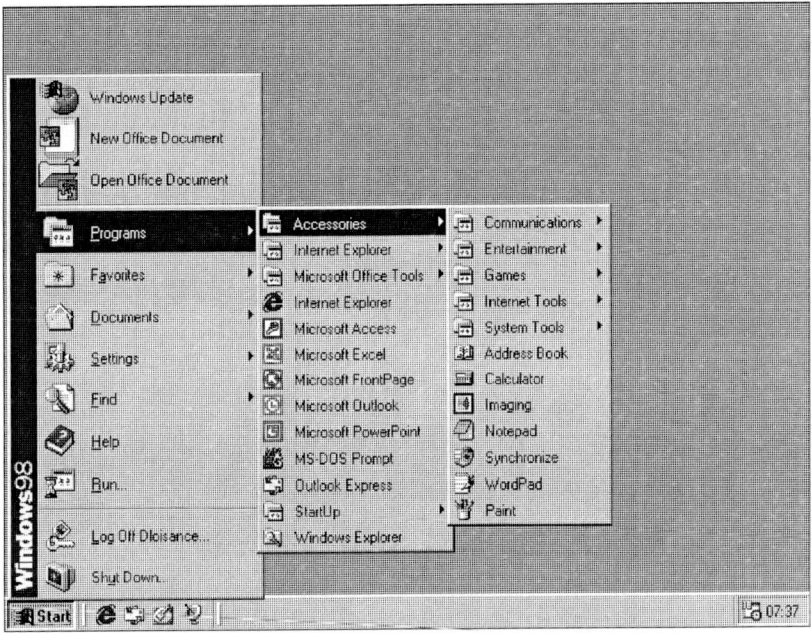

The arrow displayed to the right of some options indicates that a submenu exists for the option.

OVERVIEW

## Switching off the computer

Click the **Start** button and choose the **Shut Down** option.

> Make sure that **Shut down** is selected, then click **OK**.
>
> *To be sure that no data is lost, Windows 98 offers to save any changes made in each open document before closing it.*
>
> *The following message appear:*
>
> *It's now safe to turn off your computer.*
>
> Switch off your computer.

## Starting/Leaving an application using the Start menu

**To start an application**, open the **Start** menu then the menu or submenu containing the application. Click the application name once.

> *The application window opens. A corresponding button appears on the Taskbar.*
>
> **To leave the application**, close its window using **File - Quit** or ⊠ or `Alt` `F4`.

Windows 98

# Environment

## Switching off the computer

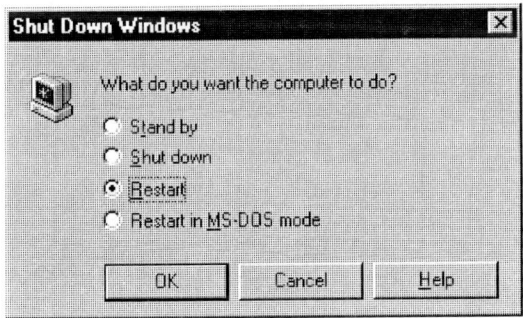

## Starting/Leaving an application using the Start menu

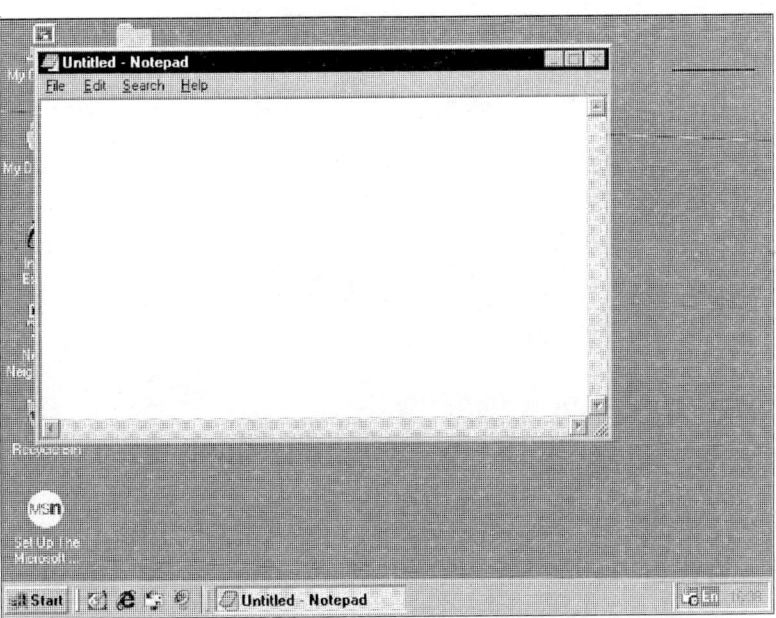

*The NotePad application is active. As you would expect, a window appears in the foreground and its button on the Taskbar seems pressed in.*

Windows 98

OVERVIEW

## Managing windows

Each window contains the following elements:
- A **Control Menu** button (a), used to manage the size or position of the window or to close it.
- A **title bar** (b) displaying the name of the active document (here, **Untitled** as no document is open) followed by the name of the application.
- The **Minimize** (c) and **Maximize** (d) buttons; the first reduces the window to a taskbar button, the second allows it to fill the whole screen.
- The **Close** button (e) closes the window (and quits the application).
- The **menu bar** (f) contains the application's various menus.
- The **scroll bars and arrows** (g) are used to scroll the contents of the window.

**To move a window**, point at the title bar (b) and drag the window to its new position (hold down the mouse and move the pointer - the window will briefly be represented by a dotted outline, but the whole window will appear in the new position when you release the pointer.)

**To close the window without shutting down the application**, click the  button (c).

*The window's name appears on the taskbar: the application is still loaded in the memory.*

**To open one of the windows on the taskbar**, click its name. The window will return to its previous size.

To hide all open windows and return quickly to the Desktop, click the **Desktop** button on the **Quick Launch** bar. To return to the window you were in before, click the button again.

## Changing the size of a window

**To enlarge a window to maximum size** and display it as full-screen, click.

**To revert to its previous size**, click (d).

**To change the width or height of a window**, drag the corresponding edge. **To change the width and height simultaneously**, drag the bottom right corner (h).

Drag the mouse until satisfied with the new size of the window; release the mouse.

16                                                                  Windows 98

# Environment

## Managing windows

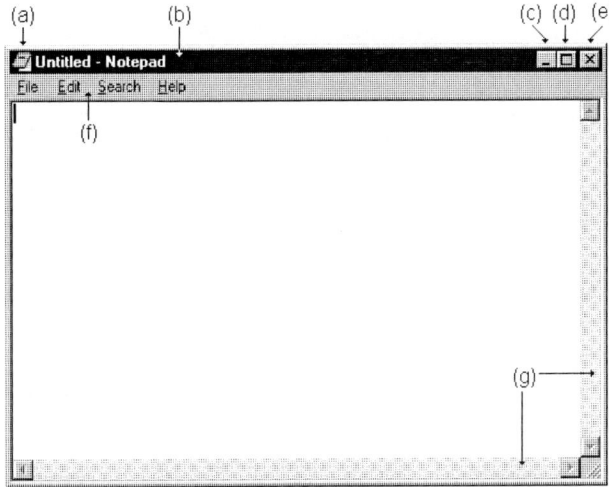

*The scroll bars are greyed out because the window is empty.*

## Changing the size of a window

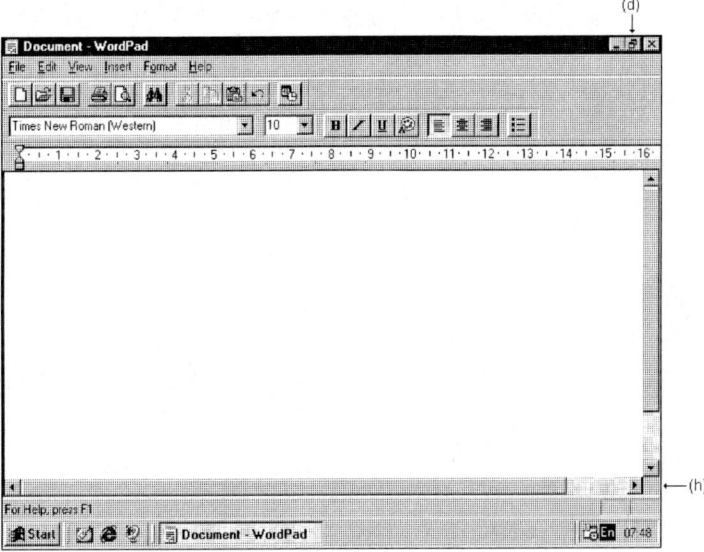

*The window fills the whole screen: only the taskbar can still be seen.*

Windows 98     17

OVERVIEW

## Managing more than one window

When you have several overlapping windows on your screen, you can tell the one which is active by its coloured title bar. Also, the corresponding button on the taskbar appears pressed in.

**To access a window** and activate the application, click in the window (if visible) or click the corresponding button on the taskbar. Alternately, press [Alt] [⇄] until the required window is activated.

*The active window appears in the foreground.*

**To change the arrangement of the windows**, right-click an empty space on the taskbar to show the taskbar menu then choose an option:

    👆 **Cascade Windows**     to have the windows overlapping

    **Tile Windows Horizontally**     to have them one above the other

    **Tile Windows Vertically**     to have the windows side by side

**To reduce all the windows to icons on the taskbar**, you can show the taskbar menu and choose the **Minimize All Windows** option.

*This choice can be cancelled by opening the taskbar menu and activating the **Undo All Minimize** option. This retrieves the last display.*

## Closing a window

Click the ☒ button or [Alt] [F4] or **File - Exit** to close an application window or [Ctrl] [F4] or **File - Close** to close a document window.

*Closing the application window means quitting the application.*

18                                          Windows 98

# Environment

## Managing more than one window

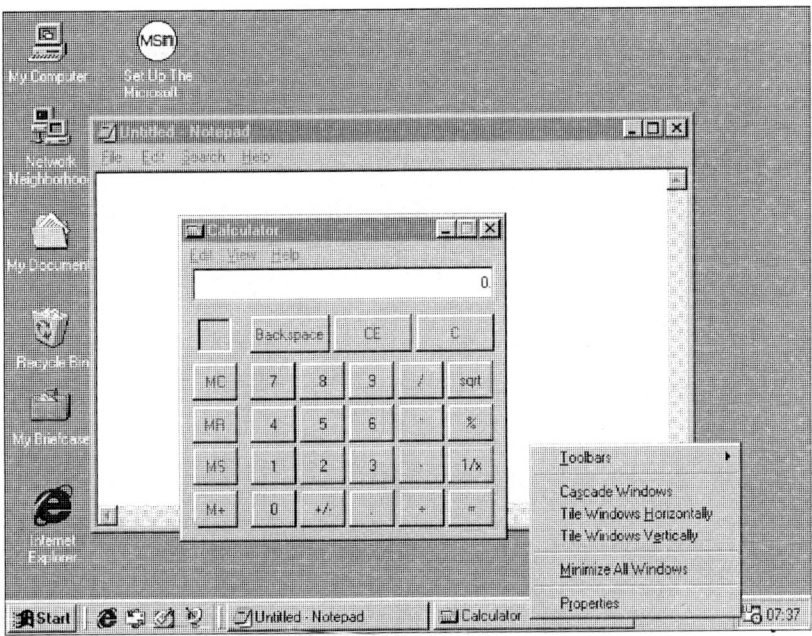

*The taskbar menu is a shortcut menu.*

## Closing a window

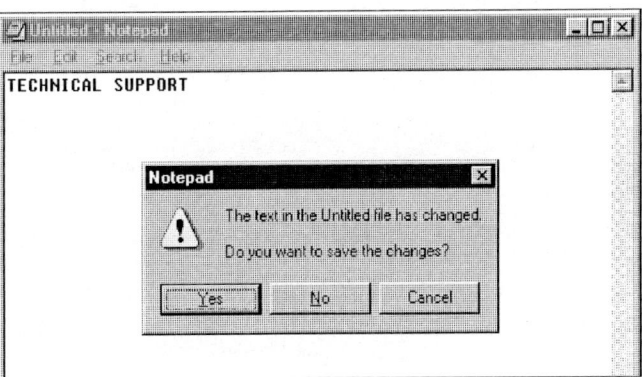

*If the application's document has not been saved, Windows offers to do so before closing the window.*

Windows 98

OVERVIEW

## Managing application menus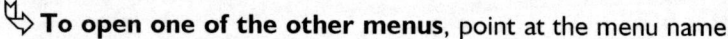

**To open a menu**, click the menu name.

*The menu options appear in the form of a list.*

> **To open one of the other menus**, point at the menu name.
>
> **To activate a menu option**, click its name.
>
> **To close the menu without using any option**, click anywhere else on the window.

## Managing application menus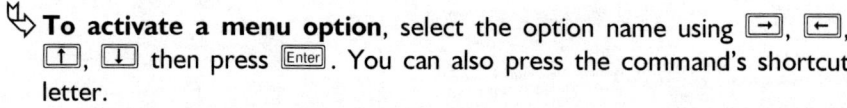

**To open a menu**, press [Alt] or [F10] to select the first menu, then press the [Enter] key to open it. Alternately, press [Alt] and the underlined letter (or shortcut letter) in the menu name.

> **To activate a menu option**, select the option name using [→], [←], [↑], [↓], then press [Enter]. You can also press the command's shortcut letter.

 The keyboard shortcuts (key combinations) you can see to the right of certain menu options allow you to choose these commands without opening the whole menu.

20                                                                Windows 98

# Environment

## Managing application menus

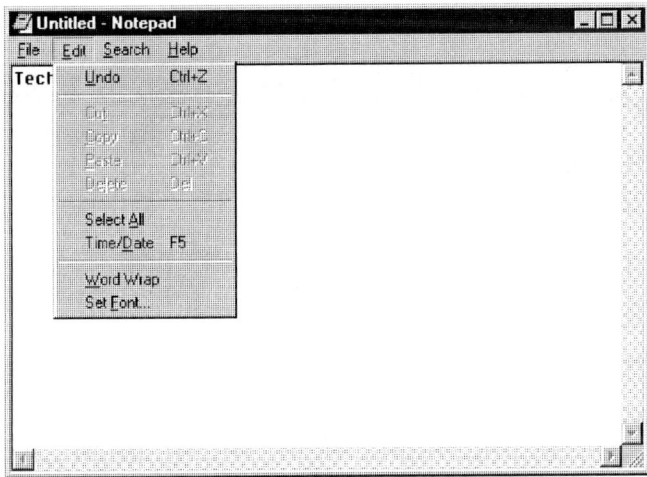

*The options which appear in grey are not currently available.*

## Managing application menus

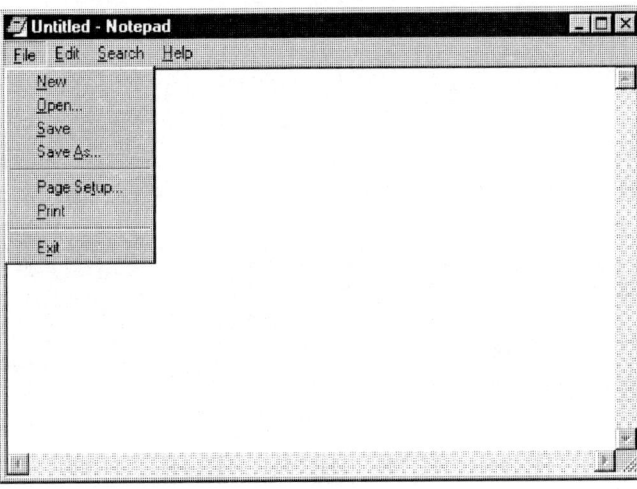

*The underlined letter on a menu or option name is a shortcut letter.*

Windows 98

OVERVIEW

## Working in dialog boxes

Dialog boxes contain some or all of the following items:
- **Tabs** (a) which open different pages.
- **Option** buttons (b): the active option's button is filled in. In an option group (like the Layout group), only one option can be active.
- **Check boxes** (c): the option is active if the box is checked.
- **List boxes** (d): this one is a drop-down list box. Click the arrow button ▼ to open the list and select an option (or click again to close the list). In a simple list box, use the scroll bars and cursors to scroll through the items in the list.
- **Text boxes** (e): type appropriate data in the text box. If the data is numerical, you may find **increment buttons** (f) which you can click to increase or decrease the value displayed.
- The OK button (g) closes the dialog box and confirms any changes you have made to the various options.
- The Cancel button (h) closes the dialog box, but does not save any changes made (clicking the ☒ button performs the same task).
- An **Apply** button (i) may appear in certain dialog boxes. Its function is to apply the defined options to the current selection without closing the dialog box.
- The [?] button (j) activates on-line help so you can obtain explanations of the various options.

> **To access an option**, use the [⇧ Shift] [⇄] or [⇄], otherwise press [Alt] and the shortcut letter for the option.
>
> **To move around inside a group of options**, or a list, use [→], [←], [↑], or [↓].
>
> **To activate or deactivate a check box**, use the space bar or click the box.
>
> **To activate another page in the dialog box**, click the corresponding tab.

# Environment

## Working in dialog boxes

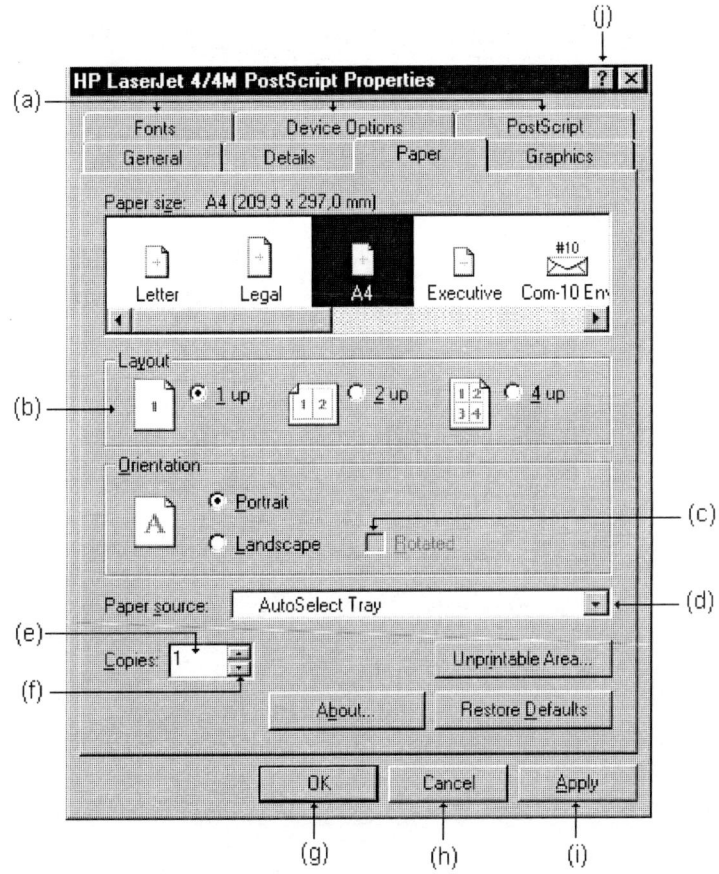

*O V E R V I E W*

## Getting help in a dialog box

**To get help**, click the ? button.

*A question mark attaches itself to the mouse pointer.*

Click the option with which you need help.

 You can also obtain help on a particular option by right-clicking it and choosing **What's this?**.

## Using the Windows help menu

Click the **Start** button and choose the **Help** option.

*The Windows Help window appears.*

In the **Contents** page, click the category which interests you and you will see the topics it contains. Click one of the topics to show the corresponding text in the help window.

On the Help toolbar, the **Back** button takes you back to the previous window, while the **Forward** button sends you to the following help window.

To **Print** the help text corresponding to the chosen topic, or the topics in the chosen category, click the **Options** button on the help toolbar and select the **Print** option.

To show or hide the table of contents, click **Show** or **Hide** on the help toolbar.

The **Web Help** button on the help toolbar allows you to obtain answers to technical questions via the Internet.

On the **Index** page, enter the first letters of the topic you are looking for, then double-click the topic to show the corresponding text.

The **Search** page will display a list of topics which correspond to the word or words you have entered in the text box.

≡24                                                                                                                                                      Windows 98

# Environment

## Getting help in a dialog box

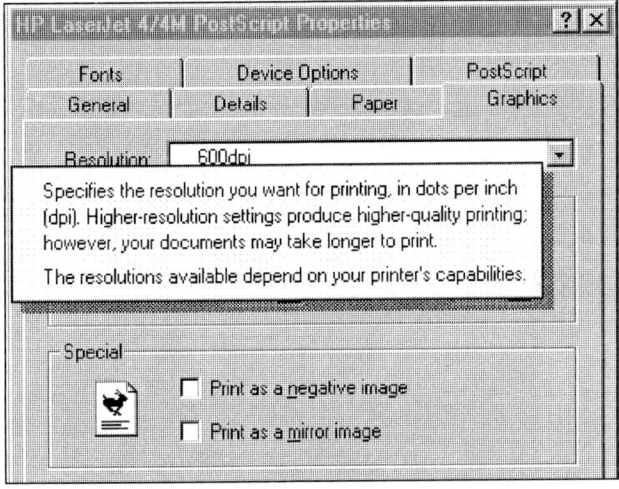

*The Help text appears in a yellow frame.*

## Using the Windows help menu

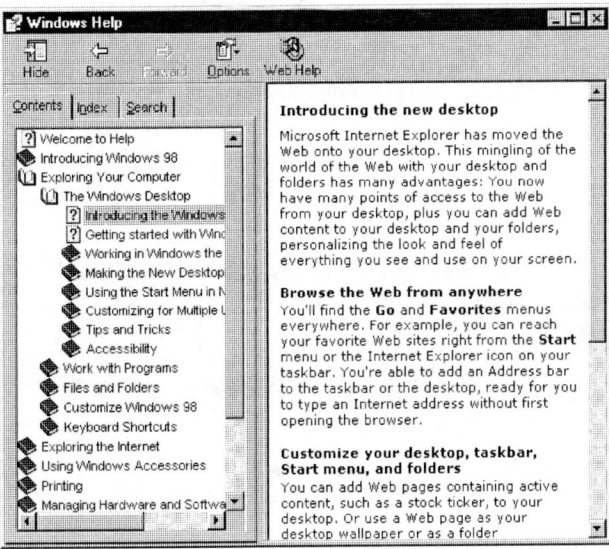

*Notice how the icons differ between a category and a topic.*

Windows 98

O V E R V I E W

## Undoing your last action

*In most Windows applications, it is possible to undo your last action.*

**Edit - Undo** or ↶ or [Ctrl] **Z**

*Some applications working under Windows (for example, Paint) allow you to undo several of your last actions.*

## Accessing drives without the Explorer

Double-click the **My Computer** icon on the Desktop.

*You will see the drives available on your workstation shown as large icons as well as the* **Control Panel, Printers, Dial-Up Networking** *and* **Scheduled Tasks** *folders.*

Point to the icon representing the required drive, then right-click.

*The drive's shortcut menu appears.*

⇨ The **Open** option opens the corresponding folder; you can also double-click the icon.

Depending on the viewing option chosen (see **Settings - Folder Options**, **General** *tab*, **Settings** *button*) the contents will appear in the active window or in a separate window.

You can manage folders and documents in this window as you would in the Explorer.

The **Explore** option starts the Explorer.

The **Find** option opens the **Find** window.

26  Windows 98

# Environment

## Undoing your last action

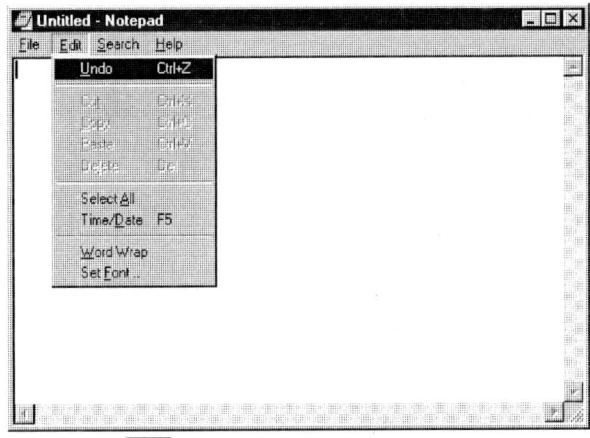

The ⤺ button is not available in *NotePad*.

## Accessing drives without the Explorer

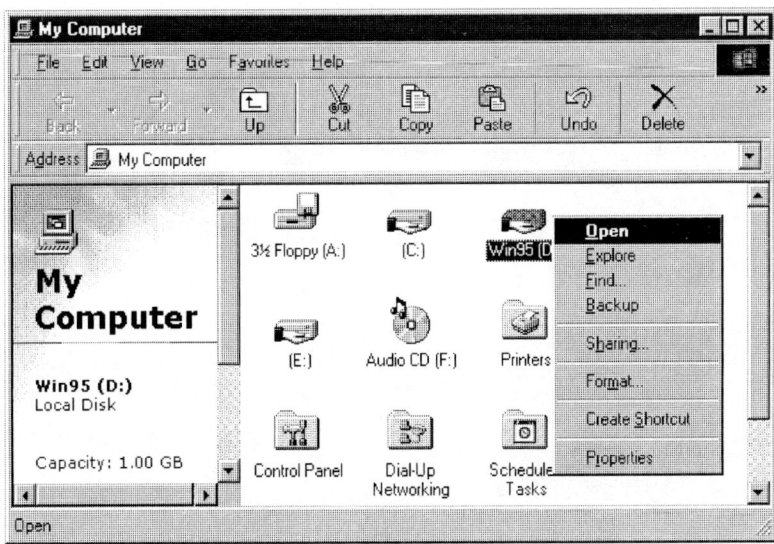

The icons shown in this window are the same as those seen in the Explorer.

Windows 98

OVERVIEW

## Accessing shared folders without the Explorer

*Several computers, installed on a network, can access the same folder when it is shared.*

Double-click the **Network Neighborhood** icon on the Desktop.

> ☞ To reach a shared folder on another workstation, double-click the workstation's name.
>
> *In the workgroup, only shared folders are accessible.*

# Environment

## Accessing shared folders without the Explorer

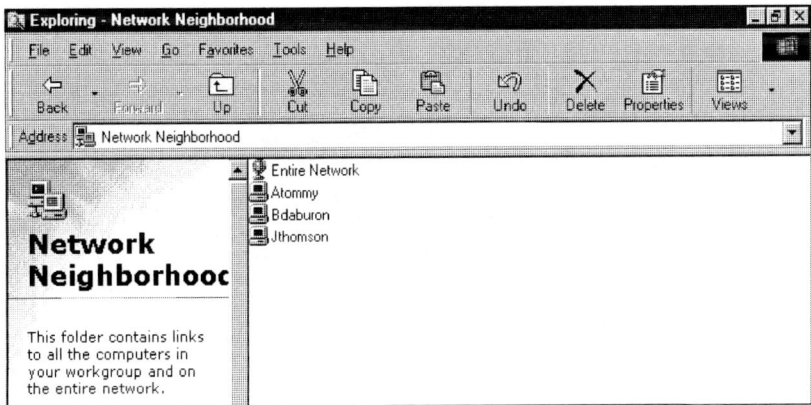

*Folders and documents can be managed here as in the Explorer.*

OVERVIEW

## Opening a document from an application

You can open a document when it has already been saved and you want to display it on the screen to read it or change it in some way.

**File - Open** or ☐ or [Ctrl] **O**

The ☐ tool and the [Ctrl] **O** shortcut are not available in every application. In some applications, it is not possible to open two documents at the same time.

⇨ Choose the drive containing the document to be opened by clicking the ▼ button on the right of the **Look in** drop-down list box (the drop-down list box's name can vary depending on the application).

Access the folder containing the document to be opened by double-clicking the yellow folder icon.

*The folder name will now appear in the Look in box.*

**To access the folder above**, click the ☐ button.

**To display a detailed list**, click ☐.

**To show a simpler list**, click ☐.

⇨ Select the document that you wish to open and click the **Open** button.

*You can also simply double-click the document to open it.*

 In certain applications, the last four documents used can be accessed using the **File** menu.

Windows 98

# Documents

## Opening a document from an application

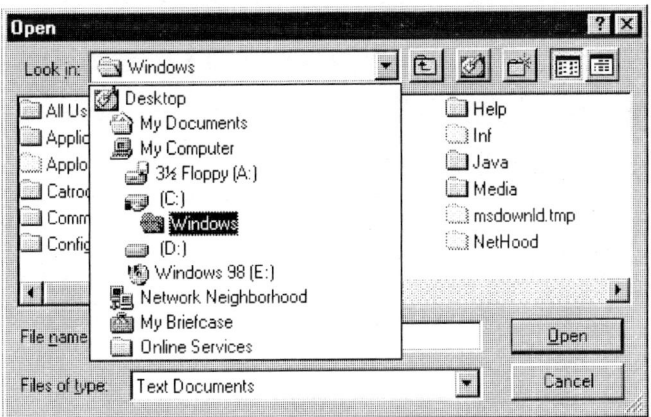

*The list contains all of the drives accessible on the workstation (the floppy disk drive (A:), the hard disk (C:), possibly additional hard disks (D:) a CD-ROM (E:) drive and the network (**Network Neighborhood**).*

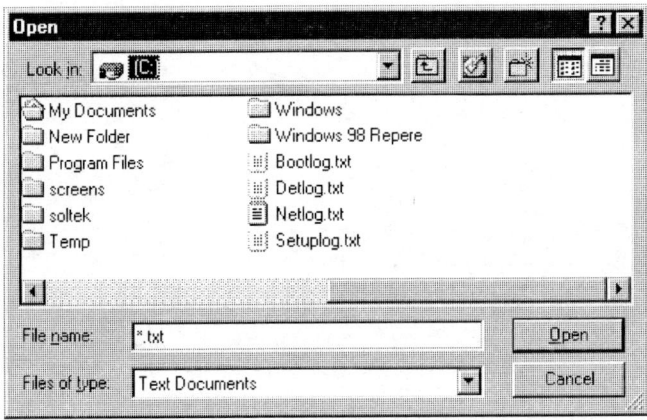

*The folder icons (the yellow ones) are different from document icons.*

Windows 98

OVERVIEW

## Opening a document from the Start menu

Click the **Start** button.

Point to the **Documents** menu.

*The last 15 documents used are listed here. It is classified in alphabetical order.*

👆 Click the document name to open it.

*Windows 98 runs the appropriate application then opens the document.*

 The **My Documents** option in the **Documents** menu lets you access the folder window containing your favourite documents.

## Creating a document from an application

File - New or  or [Ctrl] **N**

*The button and the keyboard shortcut may not be available in all applications.*

*A new document appears in the window (in the NotePad application, its default name is Untitled).*

Some applications contain document windows which allow you to manage several open documents.

# Documents

## Opening a document from the Start menu

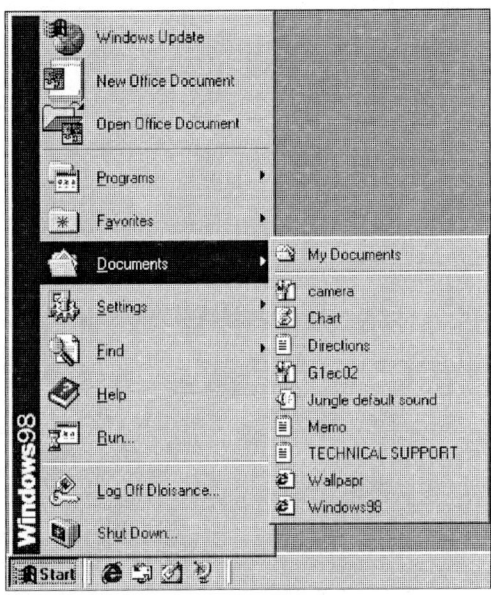

*Each document name is preceded by an icon symbolising the document type.*

## Creating a document from an application

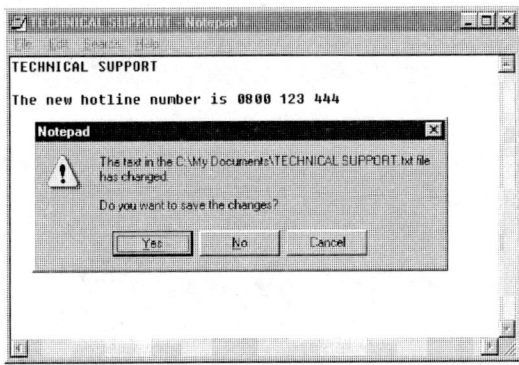

*If the application is incapable of handling several documents simultaneously, the open document will disappear from the central memory. Windows will ask whether or not to save the last changes made before closing.*

Windows 98

# OVERVIEW

## Saving a new document

**File - Save** or 🖫 or Ctrl **S**

The 🖫 tool and the Ctrl **S** shortcut are not available in all applications.

➢ **To indicate where you want to save the document**, select the drive into which the document should be saved from the **Save in** drop-down list then double-click the folder icon.

The 🖻 tool (a) lets you open the folder above.

**To name the document**, click the **File name** text box then drag to select the current name (**Untitled** for example).

Type in the name you wish to give to your new document. You may use up to 255 characters! However, the characters \ . / : " ? and | are nor permitted.

The name can contain both upper and lower case letters and spaces.

Use, if necessary, the **Save as type** list to select the saving format for the document.

Click **Save**.

The document name, and possibly its extension, appear on the title bar.

 The 📁 tool (b) will allow you to create a new folder in which to save the document if a suitable folder does not already exist.

## Saving an existing document

**File - Save** or 🖫 or Ctrl **S**

The document is saved automatically without any prompt for confirmation.

**To save a document under a different name**, use the **File - Save As** command.

The extension which follows the document's name is made up of three characters. It is connected to the file format. For example, text files often carry a TXT extension, Excel spreadsheets the extension XLS and Word documents take a DOC extension.

≡34                                                                                                       Windows 98

# Documents

## Saving a new document

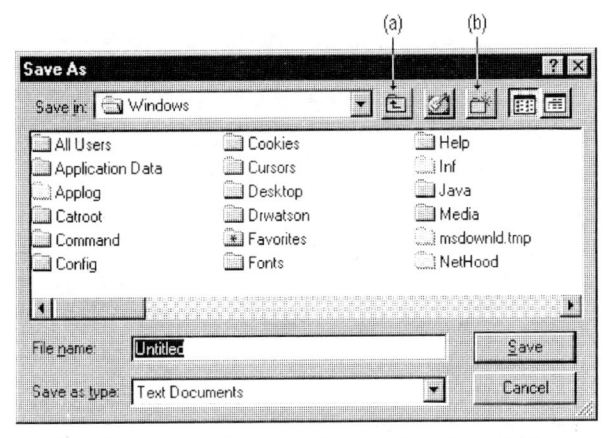

*The document will be saved in the Windows folder in a **Text Documents** format.*

## Saving an existing document

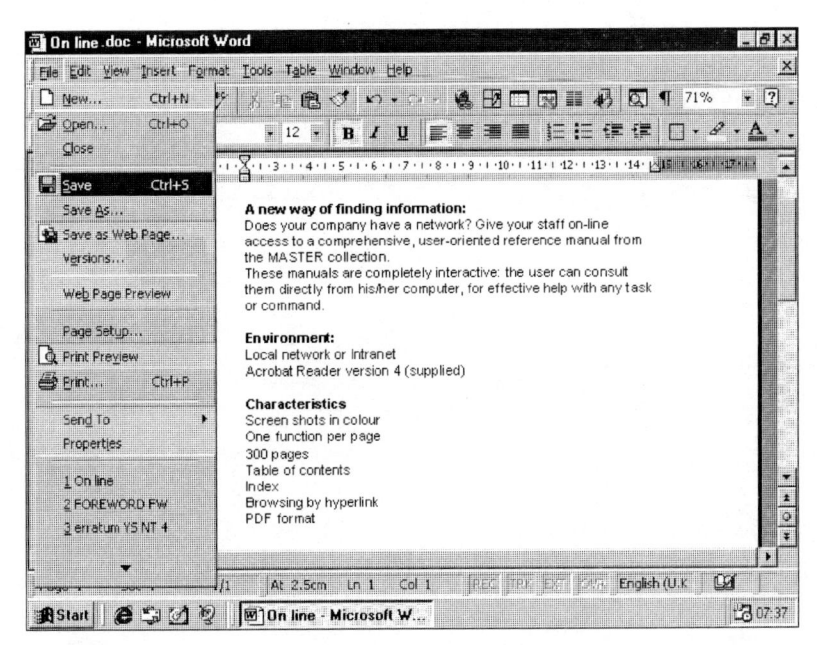

*Word documents carry a **DOC** extension.*

Windows 98

# OVERVIEW

## YOUR NOTES

# Chapter 2
## WORDPAD

- **OVERVIEW**     p.38
- **ENTERING/EDITING TEXT**     p.42
- **FORMATTING TEXT**     p.48
- **PRINTING**     p.60

# WORDPAD

## Choosing the items you need in the window

*In WordPad (word processing) you choose whether or not to display the toolbar, the Format bar and the ruler.*

**To open WordPad**, click the **Start** button, point to the **Accessories** menu and click **WordPad**.

**To change the view**, open the **View** menu.

➥ Activate the options you want to show in the window or deactivate those you do not.
- The **toolbar** (a) contains buttons whose names you can discover by pointing at them.
- The **format bar** (b) contains buttons for formatting text.
- The **ruler** (c) is used for working with margins, tabs and indents.
- The **status bar** (d) displays information concerning the task currently being performed.

## Moving the toolbar and format bar

Point to an empty space on the bar and drag to the required position.

➥ To bring the bar back to its original position, simply drag it back into place.

# Overview

## Choosing the items you need in the window

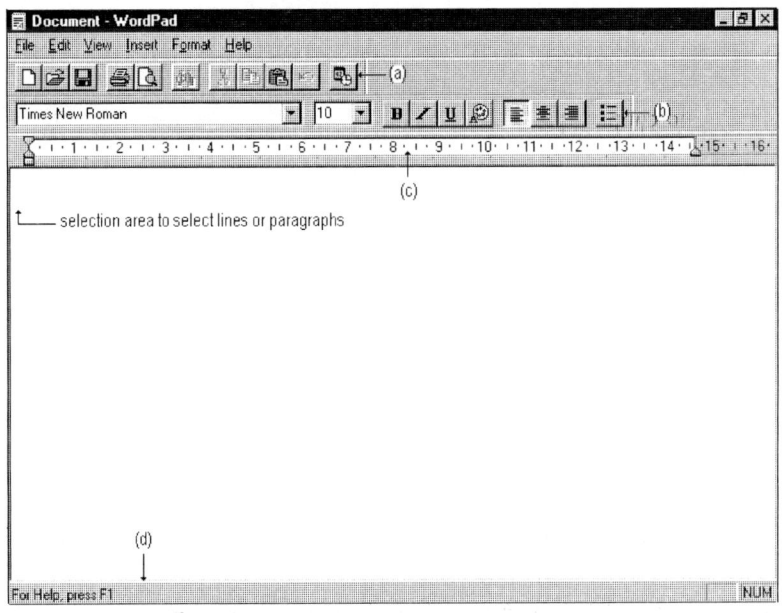

*The two toolbars, the ruler and the status bar can be seen in the WordPad window.*

## Moving the toolbar and format bar

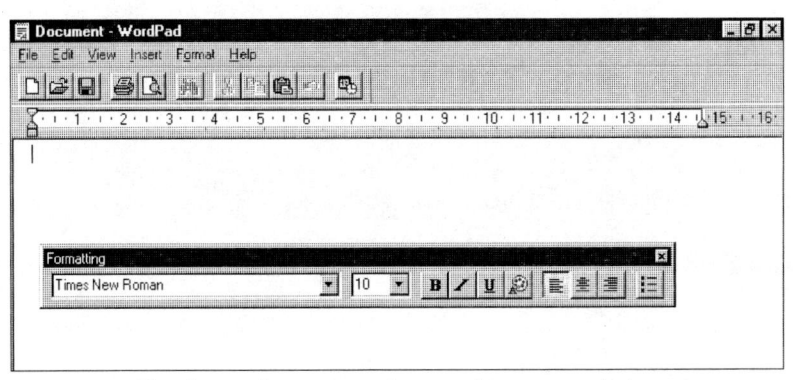

*The format bar appears here with its own title bar and a ✕ button with which to close it.*

# WORDPAD

## Moving the insertion point

*The insertion point is symbolised by a flashing bar. It shows your place in the document.*

To move the insertion point, simply click the place you wish to put it (if necessary, scroll the document with the scroll bar or cursors). You can also move it using the following keys:

| | |
|---|---|
| Next/previous character | [→]/[←] |
| Start of next word/previous word | [Ctrl][→]/[Ctrl][←] |
| End of line/start of line | [End]/[Home] |
| Next/previous paragraph | [Ctrl][↓]/[Ctrl][↑] |
| Next/previous screen | [Pg Dn]/[Pg Up] |
| Start/end of document | [Ctrl][Home]/[Ctrl][End] |

## Selecting text

If you wish to select:

| | |
|---|---|
| a word | double-click the word. |
| a line | point to the left of the line (the pointer takes the form of a black arrow, pointing up and to the right) and click once. |
| a paragraph | point to the left of the paragraph and double-click. |
| the whole document | point to the left of the text and triple-click or hold down [Ctrl] and click once. |

For a group of characters:

| | |
|---|---|
| drag | click in front of the first character to be selected then without releasing the mouse, drag across the letters you wish to select. When everything is selected release the mouse. |
| [⇧ Shift]-click | click in front of the first character to be selected, point to the last one, hold down [⇧ Shift] and click. |

*The insertion point flashes at the end of the selected text. If you right-click the selected text, the corresponding shortcut menu will appear. As a general rule, you cannot select non-adjacent blocks of text simultaneously: each one must be treated separately.*

**To cancel a selection**, click outside of it or click any arrow key.

> You can select items without the mouse by using the same key combinations you would to move the insertion point, but pressing down [⇧ Shift] at the same time (for example, [Ctrl][⇧ Shift][→] will select the next word).

Windows 98

Overview

### Moving the insertion point

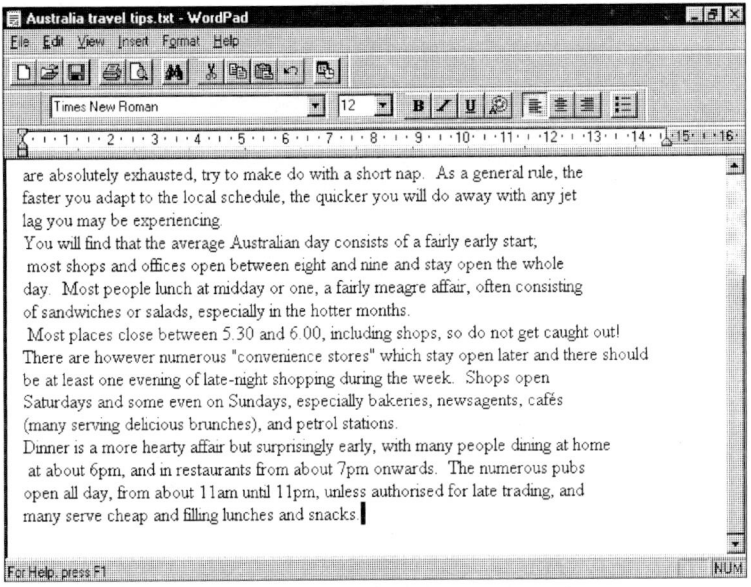

*None of the movement keys will allow you to go beyond the last character (or space) typed.*

### Selecting text

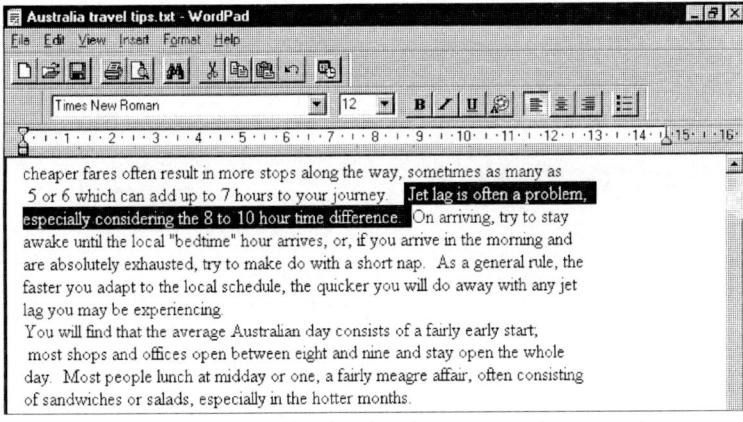

*Selected text is highlighted and any new selection will cancel the previous one.*

Windows 98

# WORDPAD

## Entering/changing text

Move the insertion point to the place where you wish to enter the text.
Type the text without worrying about the ends of the lines as WordPad will automatically bring the text onto the next line when the right margin has been passed. At the end of a paragraph, start a new one with [Enter].

*The insertion point will move down to the next line.*

**To delete text**, select the text to be deleted. Press [Del].

*The [Del] key removes the character located after the insertion point. The [←] key removes the one before it.*

**To replace text**, select the text to be replaced then type in the replacement text.

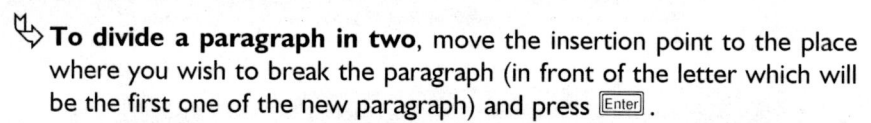

> **To divide a paragraph in two**, move the insertion point to the place where you wish to break the paragraph (in front of the letter which will be the first one of the new paragraph) and press [Enter].
>
> *This will produce two distinct paragraphs, the second one starting on the next line.*
>
> **To merge two paragraphs**, *place the insertion point in front of the first character of the second paragraph, and press* [←], *until the second paragraph joins the end of the text of the first.*
>
> *Alternatively, you can place the insertion point after the last character of the first paragraph and press* [Del].

You can include foreign characters into the text by using a combination of the [Alt] key and numbers to enter ASCII codes which will produce for example, accentuated letters not seen on your keyboard.

## Inserting the date and time

*This action inserts your computer's control time and date.*

Put the insertion point where you wish to insert the date or time.

**Insert - Date and Time** or [icon]

> Choose the format of the date or time. Click **OK**.

42                                                                 Windows 98

# Entering/editing text

## Entering/changing text

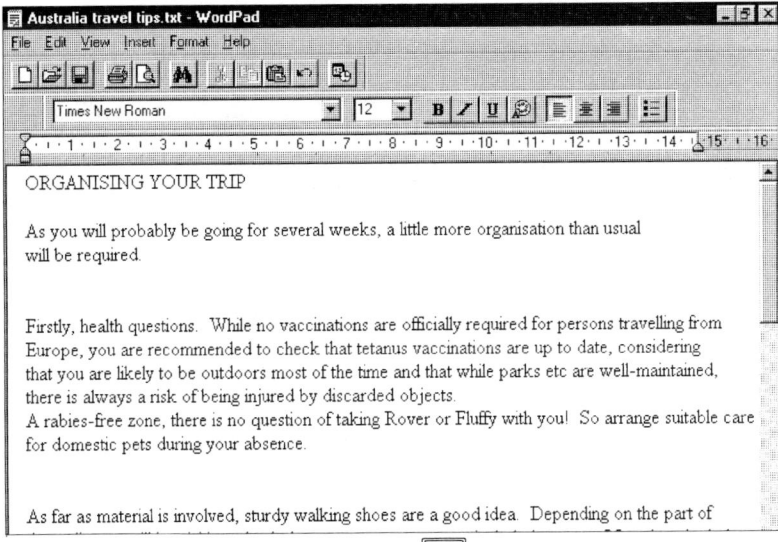

*Each blank line produced with the Enter key is also a paragraph.*

## Inserting the date and time

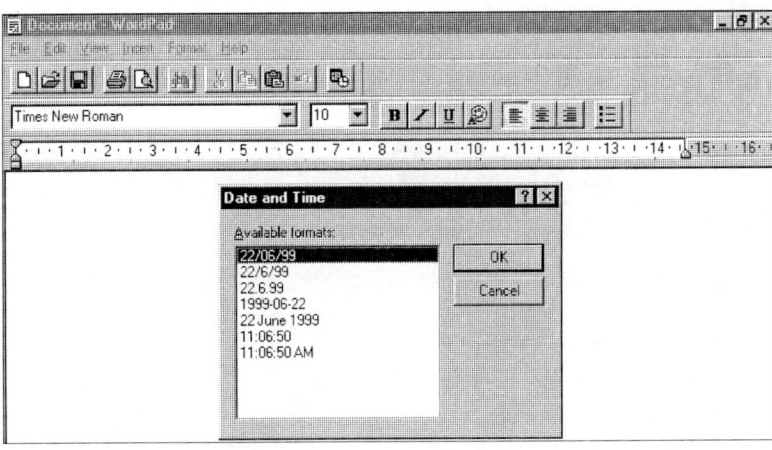

*WordPad will offer you a choice of formats for the date and time.*

# WORDPAD

## Finding text

Edit - Find... or 🔍 or [Ctrl] F

*A dialog box appears.*

> Enter the text you are looking for in the text box, then activate:

| | |
|---|---|
| **Match whole word only** | so that WordPad looks for a complete word and not a string of characters. |
| **Match case** | so that WordPad looks for the exact combination of upper and lower case letters that you have entered. |

Click the **Find Next** button to start the search.

*The dialog box stays open and it may hide the text which WordPad has found (you can move it if necessary). The search begins at the insertion point and continues to the end of the document. WordPad then searches again, from the beginning of the document up to the insertion point.*

If the text found is the one you were looking for, close the dialog box by clicking ⊠, otherwise, click **Find Next** again to continue searching.

Confirm with [Enter] or **OK**.

🔑 To continue searching once the **Find** dialog box is closed, use **Edit - Find Next** or [F3].

## Transferring text without the clipboard

*This technique lets you move text without first pasting it into the clipboard.*

Select the text to be transferred.

**To move the selected text**, drag the selection to its new location.

**To copy the selection**, hold down [Ctrl] as you drag.

When the insertion point is correctly placed, release the mouse (and [Ctrl] if used).
*The text will stay highlighted.*

# Entering/editing text

## Finding text

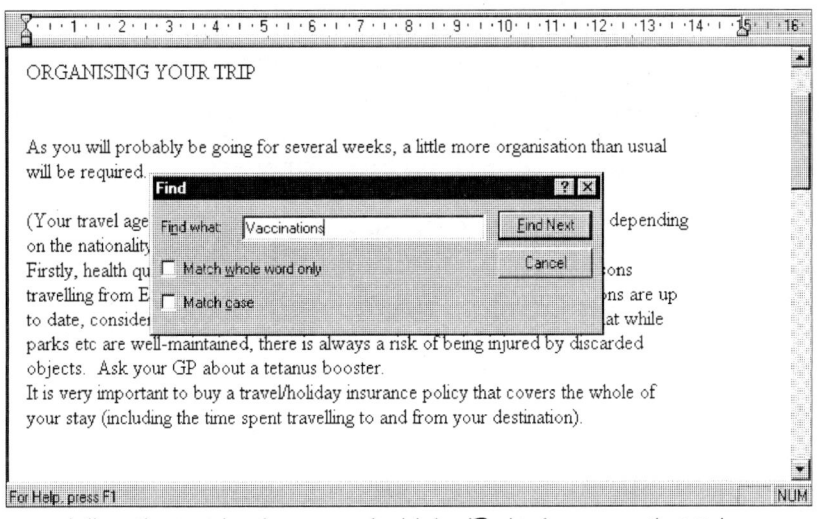

*When the text has been searched, WordPad informs you that it has completed its search.*

## Transferring text without the clipboard

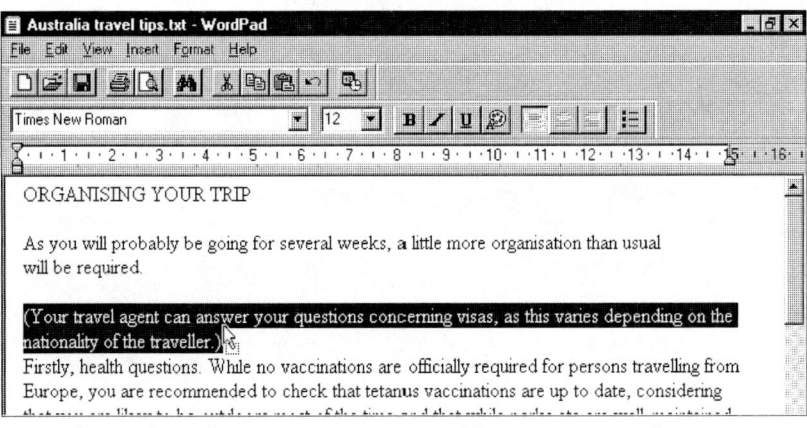

*As you drag, the pointer is accompanied by a tiny square if you are moving text or a plus sign if you are copying.*

Windows 98

45

# WORDPAD

## Replacing text

**Edit - Replace...** or [Ctrl] **H**

Enter the text to be replaced in the **Find what** box.
Enter the text to put in its place in the **Replace** box.
Activate:

**Match whole word only**   to look for the complete word and not a string of characters.

**Match case**   to look for the word exactly as you have typed it.

Click **Find Next**.

> At the first occurrence of the word, WordPad offers the following options:
>
> **Find Next**   to keep searching without changing the selected text.
> **Replace**   to replace the selected text and continue the search.
> **Replace All**   to place the word every time it occurs.
>
> When the search is completed, click **OK** then click [X] to close the dialog box.

## Copying/moving text using the clipboard

Select the text to copy or move.
**To copy the text**, use **Edit - Copy** or [icon] or [Ctrl] **C**.
**To move the text**, use **Edit - Cut** or [icon] or [Ctrl] **X**.

*The selected text is copied or moved into a temporary memory zone called the clipboard.*

Put the insertion point in the position where you wish to place the text.
*You can copy or transfer text between two documents in the same application or from another application (which manages text).*

**Edit - Paste** or [icon] or [Ctrl] **V**

*The contents of the clipboard are only temporary and change when you copy new information there. It is emptied every time you switch off your computer.*

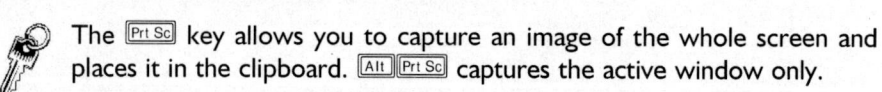

> The [Prt Sc] key allows you to capture an image of the whole screen and places it in the clipboard. [Alt][Prt Sc] captures the active window only.

≡46    Windows 98

# Entering/editing text

## Replacing text

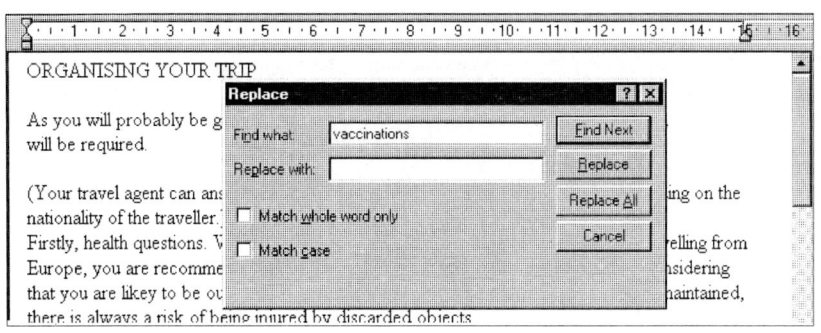

*It is possible for the dialog box to hide the word that has been found during the search!*

## Copying/moving text using the clipboard

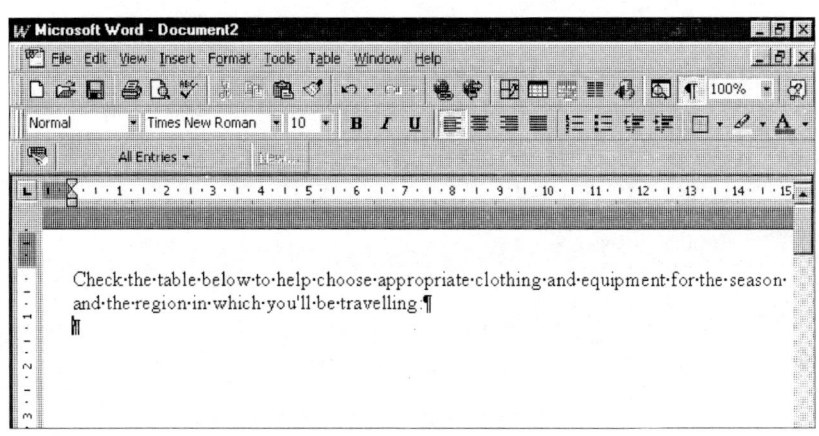

*After pasting, the selected text appears in the document. It is still contained in the clipboard and can be pasted several times if necessary.*

# WORDPAD

## Applying attributes to characters

Select the text which needs changing.

If not shown, display the format bar using **View - Format Bar**.

> Click the button corresponding to the attribute you want to apply (or remove).
>
> *The text will adopt the new attribute.*

> You can also apply character attributes using the **Format - Font** command (cf. page 52).

## Changing the font

*A font is a graphic design applied to all characters (letters, numbers, symbols...).*

Select the text.

Open the font drop-down list on the format bar.

> Click the font you wish to apply to the selected text.

> You can also change the font using **Format - Font** (cf. page 52).

Windows 98

# Formatting text

## Applying attributes to characters

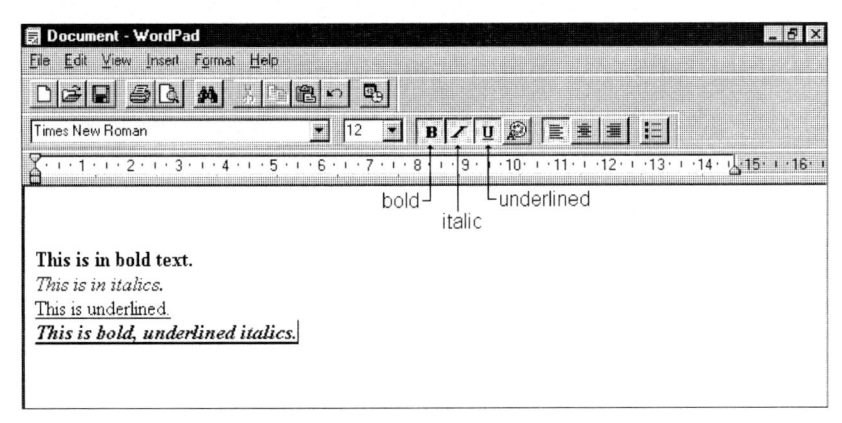

*You can apply several attributes to the same text.*

## Changing the font

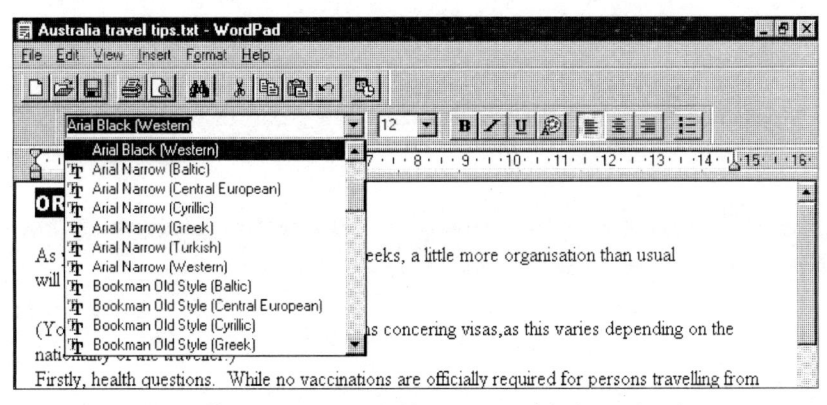

*WordPad lists the available fonts in alphabetical order.*

Windows 98

49

# WORDPAD

## Changing the font size

Select the text to be changed.

> Select the required font size from the drop-down list on the format bar.
> *The character size is expressed in **points**.*
> *As for character attributes, you can select a size before entering the text.*

> You can also change font size in the **Format - Font** dialog box (cf. page 52).

## Colouring characters

Select the characters to be coloured.

Click the ⌨ button.
*A colour palette appears.*

> Click the colour of your choice.
> Move the insertion point to see the result.

> You can also change the colour of the text in the **Format - Font** dialog box, using the **Colour** list (cf. page 52).

50  Windows 98

Formatting text

## Changing font size

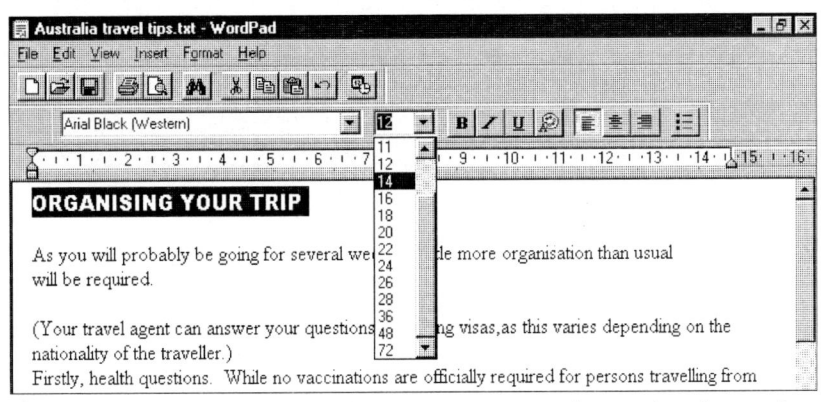

*If the size you require is not listed, you can enter it in the text box then confirm.*

## Colouring characters

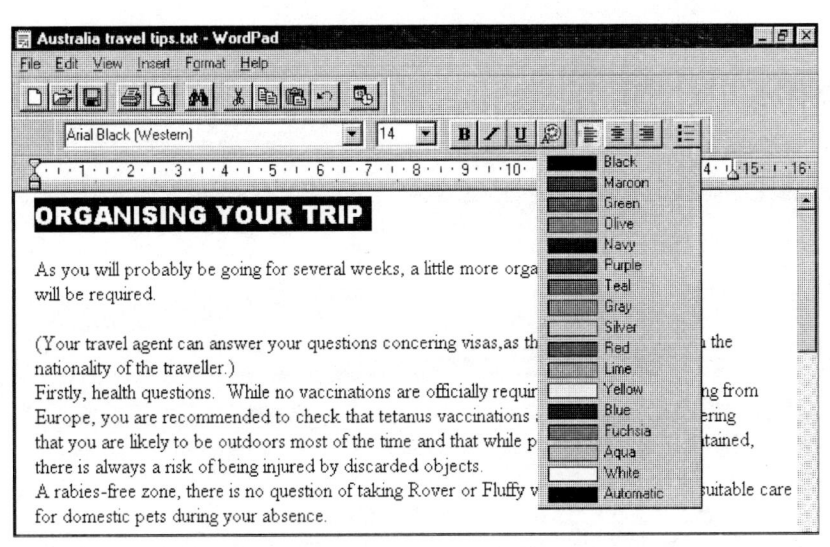

*The **Automatic** option will colour the font black.*

Windows 98

51

# WORDPAD

## Changing the character attributes font, size and colour

Select the text you wish to change.

**Format - Font**

The *Font* dialog box opens.

> Select a font, its size and colour and its style attributes in the appropriate lists.
>
> Click **OK**.

The style attributes chosen (bold, italic..) are applied to the selected text, but also to any text you may continue writing directly after. To continue writing in standard type, you must deactivate the chosen attribute.

## Changing the indents

Place the insertion point in the paragraph required or select the paragraphs.

If not shown, display the ruler using the **View - Ruler** command.

Drag the symbol of the indent you require to the appropriate point on the ruler:

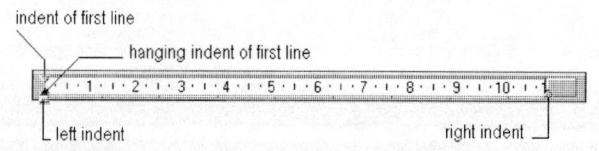

```
              indent of first line
                    ─── hanging indent of first line
        ┌·1·┬·2·┬·3·┬·4·┬·5·┬·6·┬·7·┬·8·┬·9·┬·10·┬·┐
         left indent                          right indent
```

As you are dragging, a dotted vertical line appears. When you release the mouse, the indent you requested will be applied.

Windows 98

# Formatting text

## Changing font type, size, style and colour

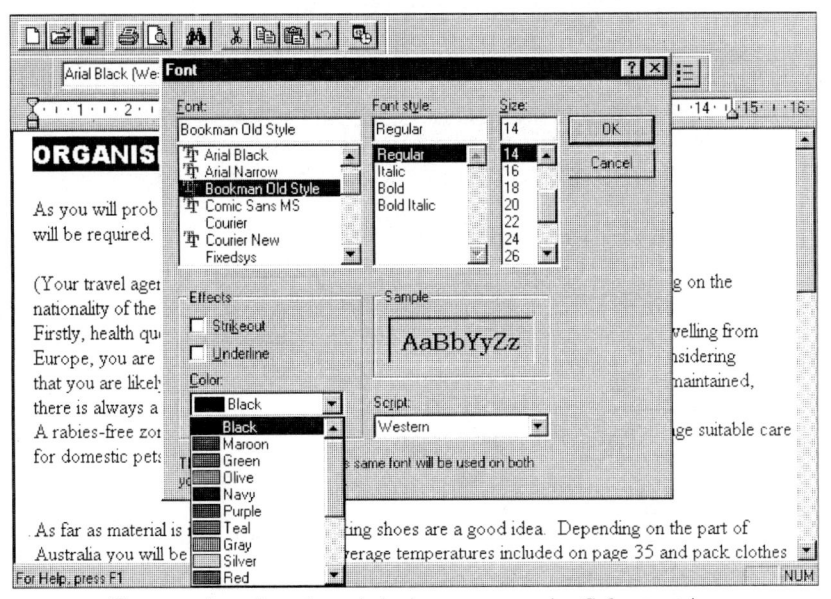

*To open the colour list, click the arrow on the Color text box.*

## Changing the indents

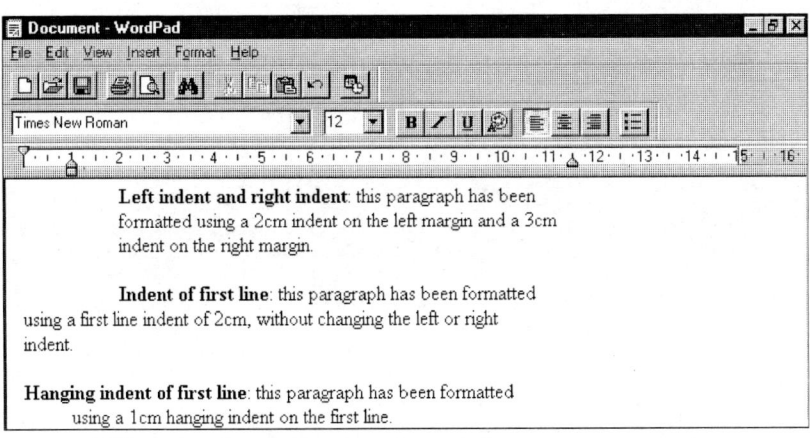

*The ruler shows the parameters of the current paragraph.*

Windows 98

# WORDPAD

## Changing the indents

Position the insertion point in the required paragraph or select the paragraphs.

**Format - Paragraph**

> Specify the indent values to apply to the paragraph(s).
> Click **OK**.

## Changing the alignment of a text

Position the insertion point in the required paragraph or select the paragraphs.

**Format - Paragraph**

> Choose the alignment you want from the list.
> *The default alignment is a left alignment.*
> Click **OK**.

> You can also use the toolbar by clicking the button to left-align, to centre and to right-align.

# Formatting text

## Changing the indents

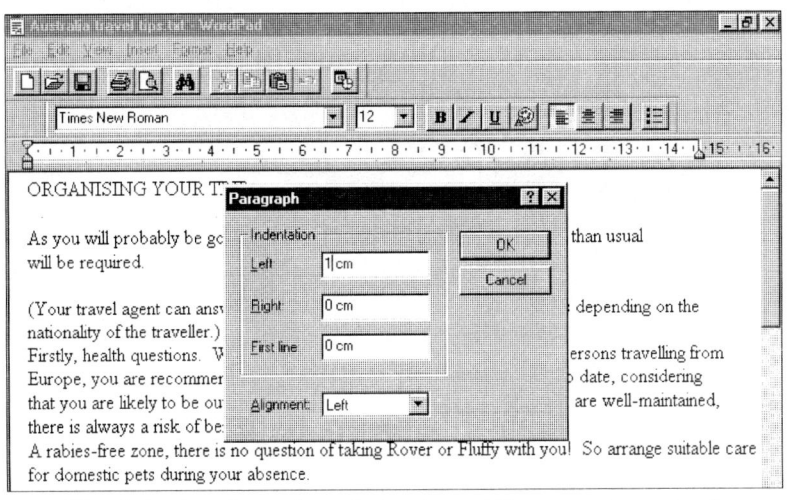

*This dialog box shows the indent values of the current paragraph.*

## Changing the alignment of a text

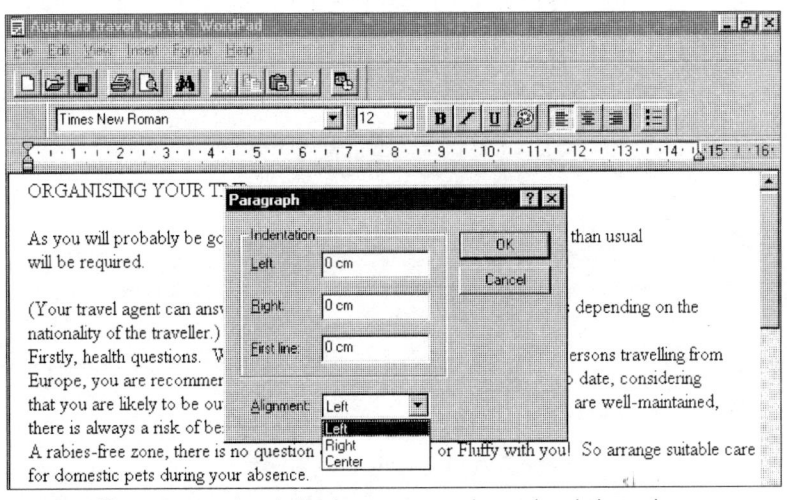

*To activate this dialog box, you can also right-click to show the shortcut menu then activate the **Paragraph** option.*

Windows 98                                                                 55

# WORDPAD

## Inserting a bullet at the beginning of a paragraph

Position the insertion point in the paragraph, if it is already created; otherwise, put the insertion point at the beginning of the new paragraph.

Click the ▦ button.

*A little circle, representing the bullet, appears.*

☞ Type the text of the paragraph (if it is a new paragraph).

*The same presentation is applied to every paragraph until you deactivate it.*

**To deactivate bullet insertion**, click ▦.

*The button will no longer look pressed in.*

## Using tabs

*Tab stops, or tabs, are used to vertically align a text. By default, WordPad sets a tab stop every 1.27 cm. They can be seen as a small grey markers along the bottom of the ruler.*

Click these keys:

⇄ to access the following tab stop,

← to access the previous tab stop.

Windows 98

# Formatting text

## Inserting a bullet at the beginning of a paragraph

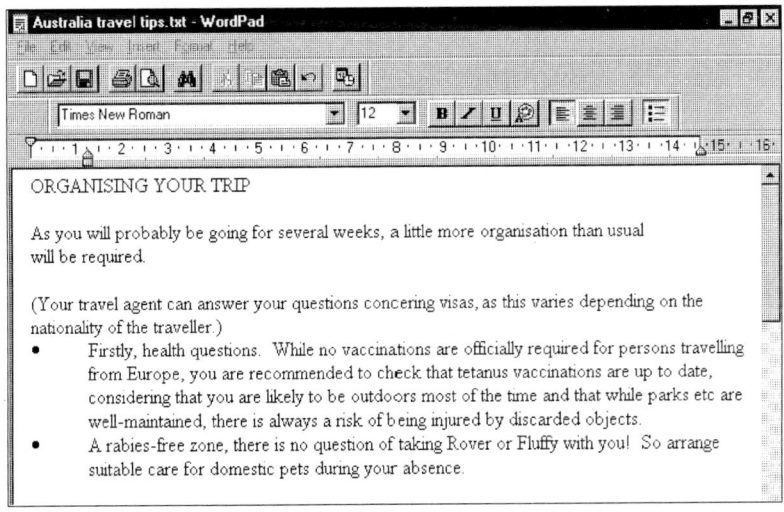

*You notice that the second line of text aligns itself with the first line. To obtain this result, WordPad has introduced a hanging first line indent.*

## Using tabs

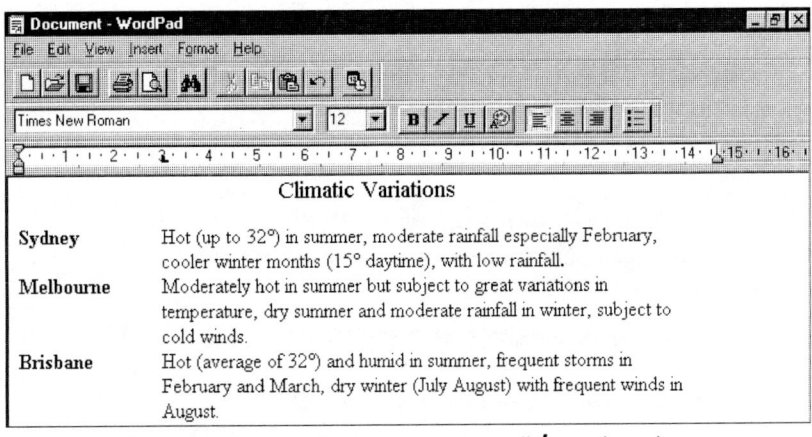

*A tab stop ou create appears as a small **L** on the ruler. It is part of the paragraph formatting: if you click outside the paragraph(s) where you set the tab, the **L** disappears.*

Windows 98

# WORDPAD

## Setting tabs

Select the paragraphs required if they are already created or position the insertion point at the required place.

**Format - Tabs...**

*The position of any tab stops previously set will appear in the list.*

☞ Indicate the position of the new tab stop in the text box.

Click **Set**.

Continue until you have defined all the tab stops.

When you have finished, click **OK**.

*These personalised tabs will replace all the default tabs that come before them.*

You can also set a tab stop by clicking the ruler at the place where you wish to position it.

## Managing tabs

**To delete a tab stop**, go into the paragraph concerned or select the paragraphs. On the ruler, point to the tab stop you want to delete.

Drag the tab stop off the ruler then release the mouse.

*The corresponding* **L** *symbol disappears.*

**To delete all tab stops**, select the paragraphs then activate the **Tabs** option in the **Format** menu. Click **Clear All** then **OK**.

**To move a tab stop**, position the pointer in the paragraph or select the paragraph.

☞ Click the tab stop you want to move and drag it into place on the ruler.

*The text aligned on this tab will move with it.*

# Formatting text

## Setting tabs

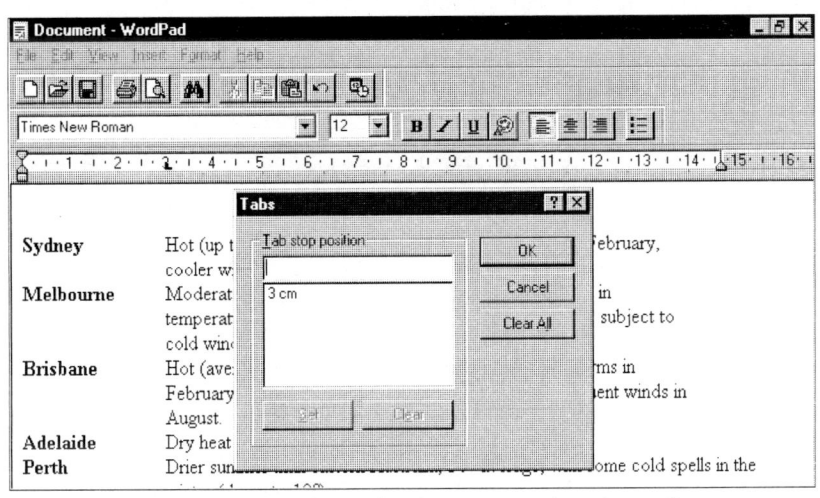

*In this example, a tab stop has been set on the ruler at 3 cm.*

## Managing tabs

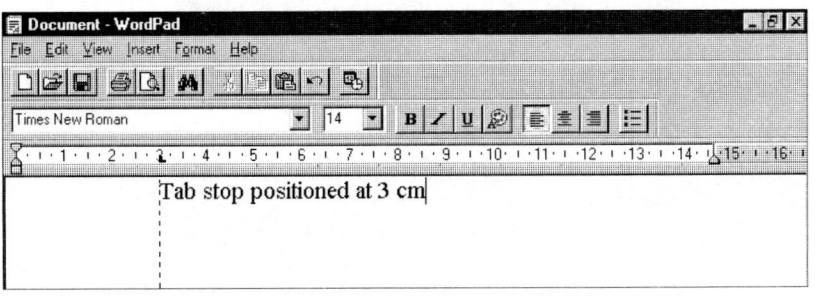

*As long as the mouse is held down, you will see a dotted vertical line.*

Windows 98 59

# WORDPAD

## Displaying a print preview

The print preview allows you to see the way your text is set out on the page before printing it.

**File - Print Preview** or 

What you see is a full page as it will appear when printed: the dotted lines represent the margins defined in WordPad. The number of the active page is shown on the status bar.

> **To magnify the preview**, click in the page or use the **Zoom In** and **Zoom Out** buttons.
>
> A vertical scroll bar appears so you can view the bottom of the page.
>
> If your document contains several pages, use the [Pg Dn] or [Pg Up] keys to look through them or click **Next Page** and **Prev Page**.
>
> **To print or modify the print parameters**, click the **Print** button.
>
> **To quit the preview**, click the **Close** button or [X] or use [Esc].

## Changing print margins and orientation

**File - Page Setup...**

The *Size* list is used to define the paper format used (by default, it uses A4).

> **To change the document's orientation**, click:
>
> Portrait      to print the page vertically
> Landscape    to print the page horizontally
>
> **To change the margins**, enter the values in the corresponding text boxes. Confirm or click **OK**.
>
> If you have changed the margins, the ends of lines will also move: on the ruler, the space reserved for text is shown in white.

> Lines will adjust themselves automatically to the margins, provided that the **Wrap to Ruler** option is activated in the **Options** dialog box (**View - Options**, **Word** tab).

# Printing

## Displaying a print preview

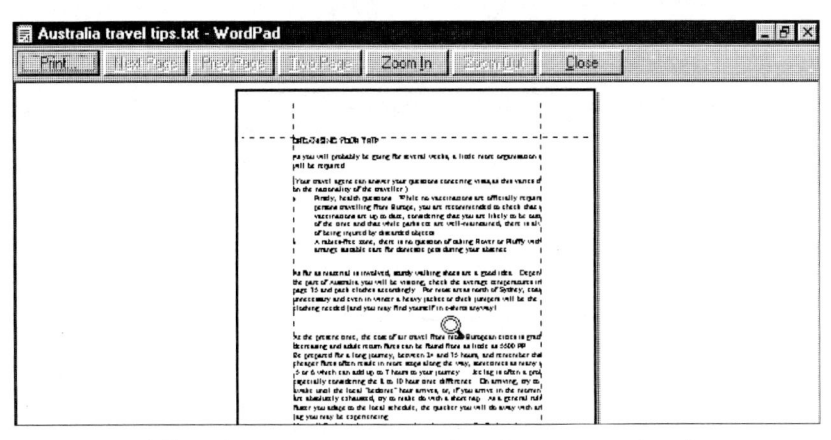

*When the pointer is positioned on the page, it takes the form of a magnifying glass.*

## Changing page margins and orientation

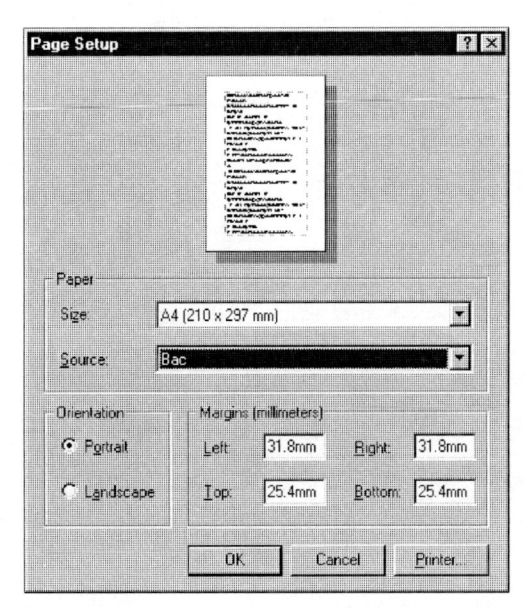

*Depending on the printer installed, it is not always possible to reduce the margins beyond a certain point.*

# WORDPAD

## Printing a document

File - Print... or Ctrl P

⇨ **To print the whole document**, check that the All option is activated.

**To print a specific group of pages**, activate the Pages option then enter the numbers of the first and last pages in the from and to text boxes.

**To print several copies**, enter the number required in the Number of copies box.

*If your printer allows, activate the Collate option to print all copies of one page, then all copies of the next page...*

Click **OK** to start printing.

*WordPad sends the document to the Print Manager: as long as the dialog box stays open, you can still cancel printing.*

**To print part of a text**, select the part you want to print, open File - Print the click Selection. Confirm with OK.

**To pause or cancel printing**, open the print manager window by double-clicking the 🖨 icon on the bottom right of the screen (on the taskbar) as long as the document has not finished printing.

*You will have to be quick, as sending documents to the print manager does not take very long!*

⇨ Click the name of the document then **Printer - Pause Printing**.

🔑 The 🖨 button starts printing directly, using the previous parameters set (no dialog box will open).

62  Windows 98

# Printing

## Printing a document

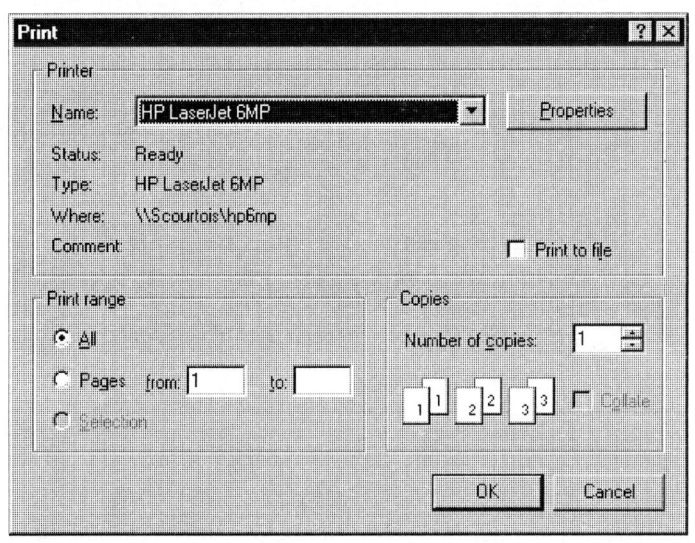

*The **Properties** button opens a dialog box allowing you to define, among other things, the paper format used and the page orientation.*

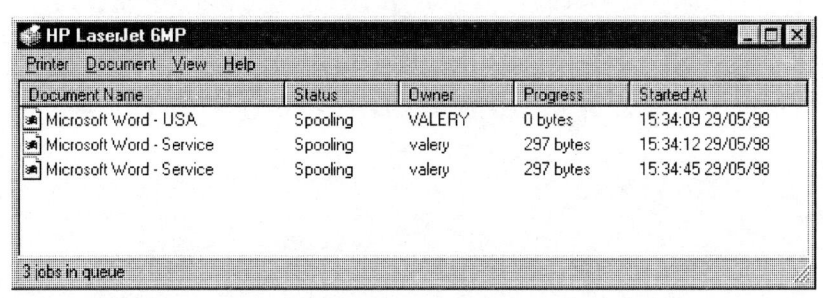

*The documents to be printed are listed chronologically. You can change the printing order by dragging a document name to a different position on the list.*

Windows 98

# WORDPAD

## Managing the print queue

**To open the Print Manager window**, double-click the **My Computer** icon on the desktop. Open the **Printers** folder then double-click the icon corresponding to your printer.

*If you have just started printing, you can also double-click the 🖶 icon seen on the right side of the taskbar.*

> **To interrupt printing**, right-click the document's name then activate the **Pause Printing** option. To restart printing of the document, deactivate the option.
>
> **To move a document up or down the queue**, which makes it print before or after other documents, click its icon and drag it up or down.
>
> *If you are printing across a network, you can only change the document's position in the queue from the workstation to which the printer is connected.*
>
> **To cancel printing a document altogether**, right-click the document name then choose **Cancel Printing**.
>
> **To cancel all printing jobs**, use the **Printer - Purge Print Documents** command.
>
> *Again, for a network printer, you must use the workstation to which the printer is connected.*

# Printing

## Managing the print queue

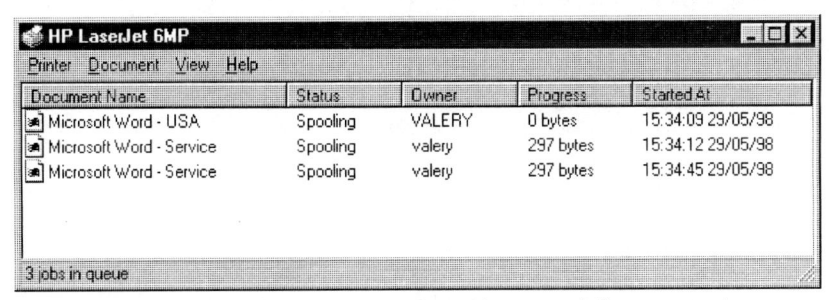

| Document Name | Status | Owner | Progress | Started At |
|---|---|---|---|---|
| Microsoft Word - USA | Spooling | VALERY | 0 bytes | 15:34:09 29/05/98 |
| Microsoft Word - Service | Spooling | valery | 297 bytes | 15:34:12 29/05/98 |
| Microsoft Word - Service | Spooling | valery | 297 bytes | 15:34:45 29/05/98 |

3 jobs in queue

You can see the list of documents waiting to be printed. On a network printer, the list also contains all documents sent by other workstations using the same printer.

# WORDPAD

## YOUR NOTES

# Chapter 3
# PAINT

- **OVERVIEW**     p.68
- **MAKING A DRAWING**     p.72
- **EDITING A DRAWING**     p.80

# PAINT

## Looking at the Paint window

The Paint window contains the following items:
- the **image area** (a) is the space where you can create your artwork.
- the **tool box** (b) contains the tools which help you create and manage your drawings; the selected tool's button seems pressed in (as here with the Erase tool).
- the **option box** (c) can contain options relating to the tool being used: for the Erase tool for example, you can change the size of the eraser.
- the **color box** (d) contains a choice of colours for the foreground (e) and background (f). The selected colours are displayed to the left of the box.
- the **status bar** contains a help message display (g) as well as an indicator of the pointer's position in the image area (h) and an indicator of the image's dimensions (i).

## Moving the tool box or the color box

Point to an empty space on the tool box or color box and drag to the required position.

*The tool box appears with a title bar and a* ☒ *button to close it.*

To return the tool box to its original position, drag it back.

Windows 98

# Overview

## Looking at the Paint application window

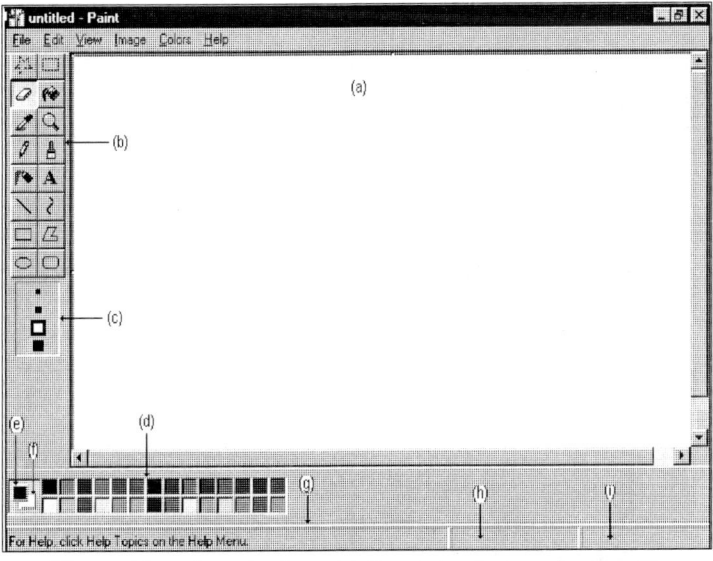

*The tool box, the color box and the status bar can be seen if the corresponding options in the View menu are activated.*

## Moving the tool box or the color box

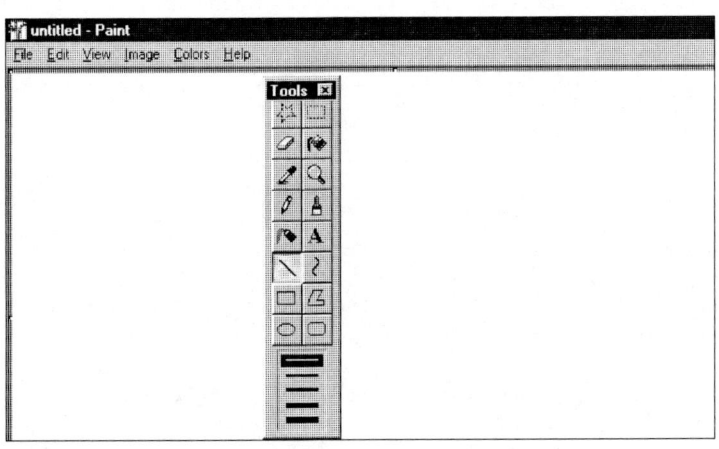

*You actually drag a dotted outline representing the tool or color box, which you use to find the correct position; the "real" tool or color box will take its place when you release the mouse.*

Windows 98

# PAINT

## Changing the size of the image area

*This technique allows you to change the height and width of the area which will contain your drawings.*

Point to one of the handles visible around the image area. Point to a corner handle if you wish to change height and width simultaneously.

*The pointer takes the form of a two-headed arrow.*

Drag the mouse in the desired direction.

*While you drag, the image area's dimensions are shown on the status bar.*

> To give the image area an exact size, enter the desired width and height in the **Attributes** option in the **Image** menu then click **OK**.

## Creating a drawing

A drawing is created in 3 stages.

### Select a drawing tool

Click the button corresponding to the tool on the tool box.

*Depending on the tool selected, a choice of options may appear in the options box underneath the tool box.*

If necessary, select one of these options.

### Select the drawing's colours

Point to the desired colour on the color box. LEFT-click to define a foreground colour and RIGHT-click to define a background colour.

### Make the drawing

Make the drawing by dragging with the left mouse button to draw it in the foreground colour, or the right mouse button to draw it in the background colour.

> To display the image area across the whole screen, use **View - View Bitmap** (or press **Ctrl F**). Click in the image area to return to the usual screen.

# Overview

## Changing the size of the image area

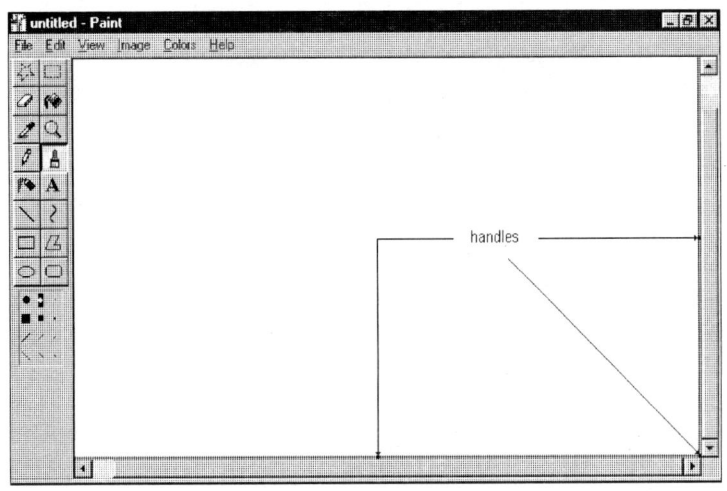

*The scroll bars become visible if the image area is larger than the window*

## Creating a drawing

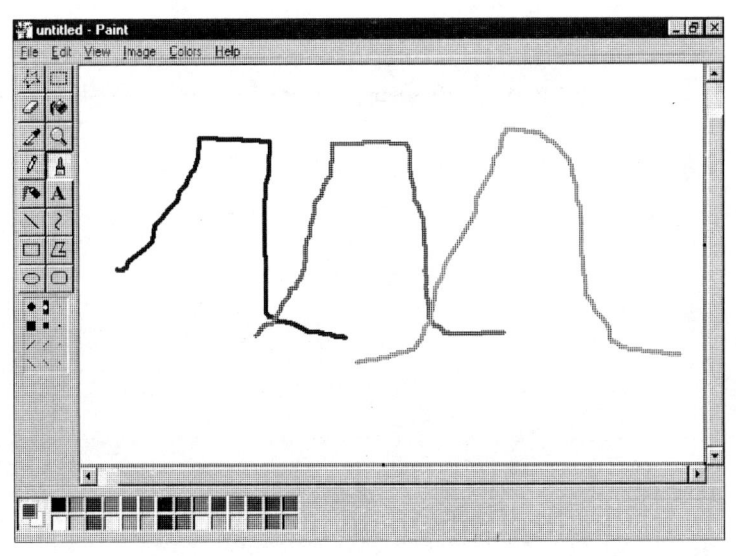

*The foreground and background colours can be seen in the small squares to the left of the color box.*

Windows 98

# PAINT

## Drawing a rectangle, a square, a circle or an ellipse

Select a tool:

| □ | to draw a right-angled rectangle |
| ◻ | to draw a rounded rectangle |
| ⬭ | to draw a circle or an ellipse |

*This will activate the options box.*

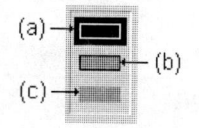

(a), (b), (c) — The options box gives you a choice between an empty rectangle (a), a coloured rectangle with a solid outline (b), or a coloured rectangle with no outline (c).

Select the type of shape you wish to draw.

Select the colours for your drawing.

Point at the place on the image area where you want to make the drawing.

Click, then drag to the opposite corner. Release the mouse when the shape is the right size.

> To draw a perfectly proportioned square or circle, hold down ⇧ Shift while you drag.

# Making a drawing

## Drawing a rectangle, a square, a circle or an ellipse

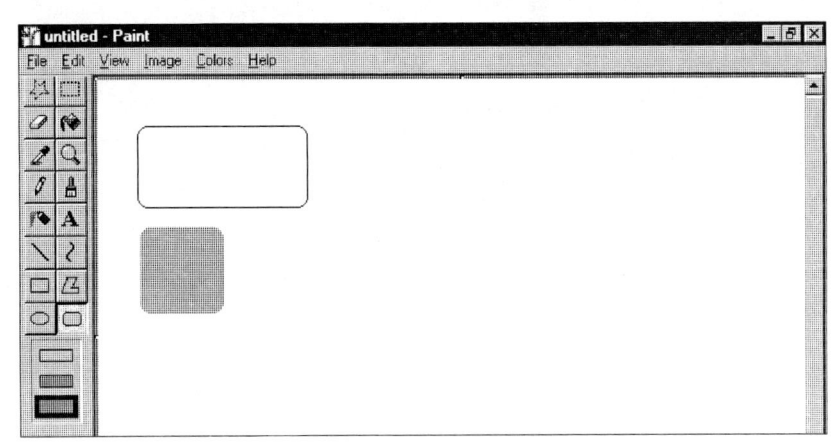

*The figure's outline appears in the selected foreground colour and it is filled in with the chosen background colour.*

PAINT

## Drawing a straight line or a curve

**To draw a straight line**, click ▨.

Select the line thickness in the options box.

Select the drawing's colour.
*With straight lines, the background colour is irrelevant.*

Position the pointer in the image area.

Click, then drag and release when the drawing is completed.
*To draw a line which is perfectly vertical or horizontal, or an oblique line at 45°, hold down the* ⇧Shift *key while you draw, release the mouse then release* ⇧Shift.

**To draw a curve**, select the ▨ tool.

Select the curve's thickness in the options box.

Select the drawing's colour (foreground colour).

Position the pointer in the image area.

Drag to draw a line linking the two ends of the curve.

Click the line you have drawn and drag upwards or downwards to make it curve.

☞ Click again and drag in the opposite direction to draw a second curve.
*Until you release the left mouse button a second time, you can erase the curve by right-clicking.*

# Making a drawing

## Drawing a straight line or a curve

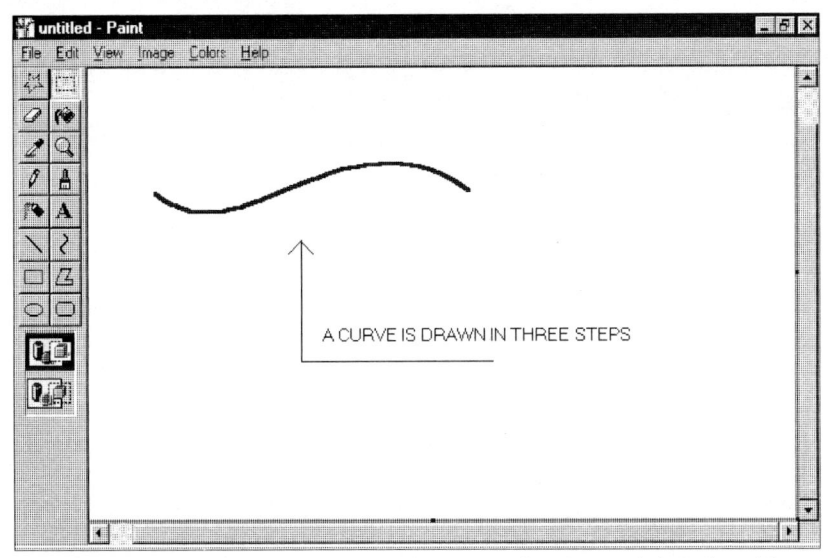

Once the original line is drawn, you have two chances to click and modify the curve. If you click a third time, Windows assumes you want to draw another curved line.

PAINT

## Drawing polygons

**To draw a triangle**, select the ▱ tool.

Select, in the option box, the type of shape you want to draw.

Select the drawing's colours.

Position the pointer in the image area.

Drag to draw one of the sides of the triangle.

Position the pointer where the third corner should be.

Double-click this corner to close the triangle.

> For the base line you are drawing to be perfectly horizontal, vertical or at a 45° angle, hold down ⇧Shift while drawing.

**To draw any polygon**, select the ▱ tool then the drawing's colour.

Draw the first side of the polygon.

Click the position of the second corner.

Click each corner in the same way.

To close the polygon, double-click the first corner.

*As long as the polygon is not closed off, you can erase it by right-clicking.*

# Making a drawing

## Drawing polygons

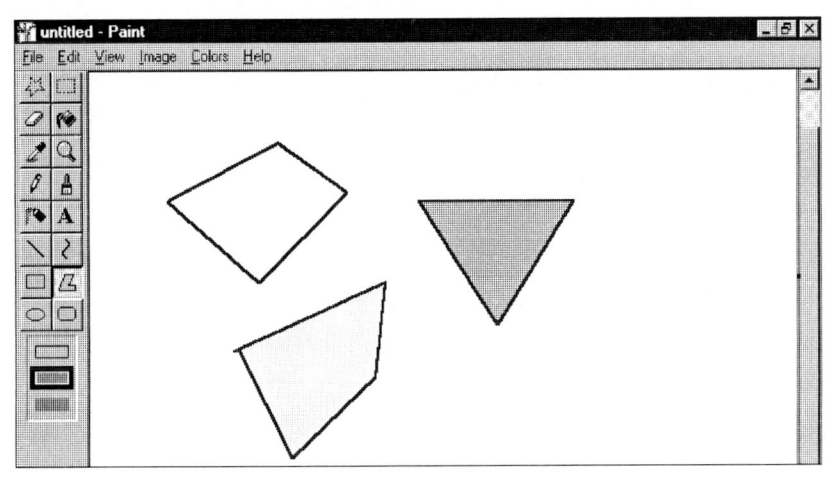

*A triangle is a three-sided polygon.*

# PAINT

## Managing text

**To enter text**, select the [A] tool.

Select the option:

[icon] to colour the background of the text box in the background colour.

[icon] to make the text box background transparent.

Select the foreground colour to apply to the text. Select the background colour if you have chosen the [icon] option.

Position the pointer in the image area.

Click at the place where you wish to start entering text and drag to draw the text box.

*An insertion point flashes inside a text box surrounded by handles. Drag one of these handles if you want to modify the size of the text box.*

☞ Type in the first line of text.

*The text will have the attributes defined in the Text toolbar.*

Press [Enter] to change line. The insertion point will move to the next line.

Continue entering the text in this way.

**To erase the text**, as long as you have not clicked outside the text box, you can use [←].

*If you have already clicked outside the text box, you will have to use the Erase tool and rub out the text as you would a drawing.*

**To alter your text's presentation**, while you are entering it, use the options on the **Text** toolbar.

*The chosen parameters will be applied to all the characters in the text box.*

When you have finished entering the text, and it is displayed in a correct style, click anywhere outside the text box.

*You can no longer modify the text or its presentation style.*

# Making a drawing

## Managing text

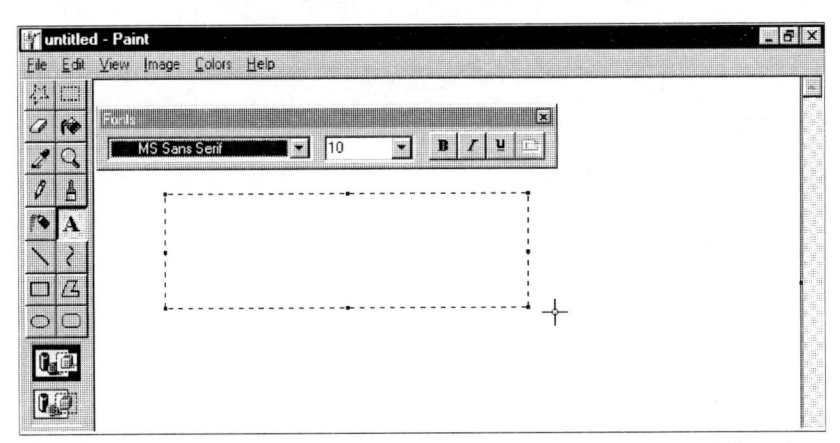

A "floating" toolbar appears when you draw the text box (provided that the
**View - Text Toolbar** option has been activated).

# PAINT

## Erasing a drawing

**To erase part of a drawing**, select the [✏️] tool.

In the option box, select the size of the eraser.

*Rubbing out a drawing actually covers it with the chosen background colour.*

By default the erased zone takes the background colour. Ensure that an appropriate background colour has been chosen.

Drag the eraser symbol over the area you wish to erase.

*The drawing can be brought back using the Edit - Undo command.*

**To erase the drawing in its entirety**, use Image - Clear Image (or [Ctrl][⇧ Shift] **N**).

🔑 You can also erase a drawing by selecting it with the [✂️] or [▭] tools and pressing [Del].

## Moving a drawing

Select the drawing you want to move.

Check that the background colour is the same as that used to fill the drawing.

Position the pointer inside the selection.

*The pointer takes the form of a cross with four arrowheads.*

👆 Drag to move the selection to its new position.

Use *Edit - Undo* to cancel the move.

Windows 98

# Editing a drawing

## Erasing a drawing

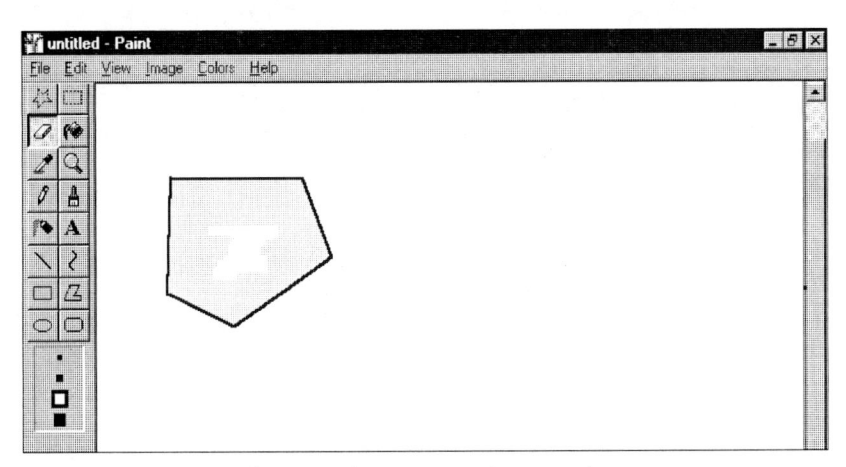

*The erased zone is seen here in white.*

## Moving a drawing

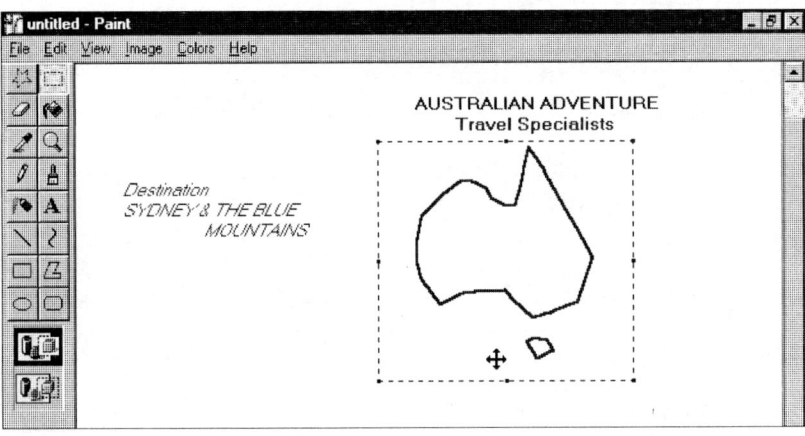

*Ensure that the pointer takes this form before dragging the selected items.*

# PAINT

## Selecting part of the image

If the part to be selected can be contained in a rectangle, choose the ▭ tool.
If the shape is irregular, choose ▦.

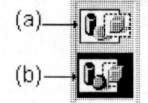

(a) —
(b) —
The options box allows you to make an opaque (a) or a transparent (b) selection.

If you want uncoloured areas of the selection to remain colourless when the selection is transferred onto the coloured background, choose opaque (1st option). If you prefer that these areas adopt the colour of their destination, choose transparent (2nd option). Drag to enclose the area you are selecting.

A dotted border encloses the selection. The handles seen on this border do not have the usual function of resizing the selection box, but instead they deform the image contained within it.

Right-click inside the selection box to display the shortcut menu.

➥ Left-click outside the menu, but inside the selection box to close the menu.
To deselect what you have selected, click anywhere outside the selection box or press [Esc].

## Copying an image inside the image area

Select the drawing concerned.

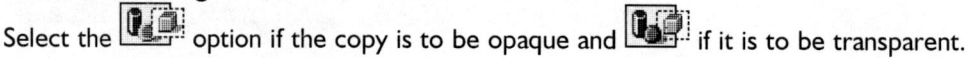

Select the ▦ option if the copy is to be opaque and ▦ if it is to be transparent.

Position the pointer inside the selection.

*The pointer will take the form of the cross with four arrowheads.*

➥ Press [Ctrl] and hold it while you drag to move a copy of the drawing.

🗝 If you hold down the [⇧ Shift] key instead of [Ctrl], you will create a multiple copy effect.

Windows 98

# Editing a drawing

## Selecting part of the image

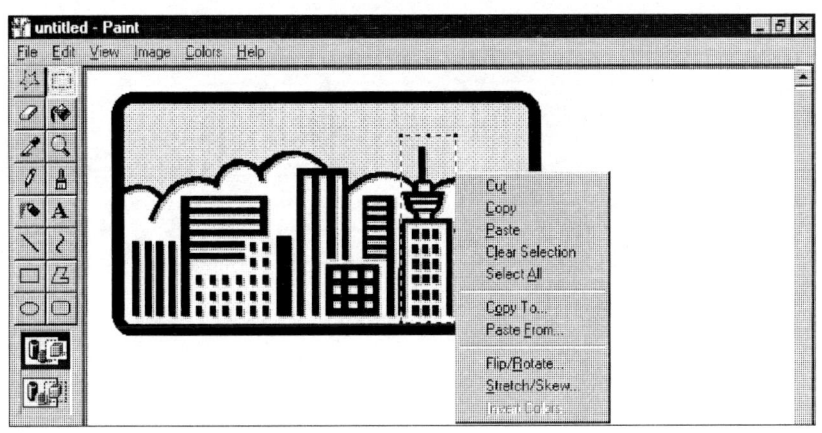

*The shortcut menu's options can also be found in the Edit and Image menus.*

## Copying an image inside the image area

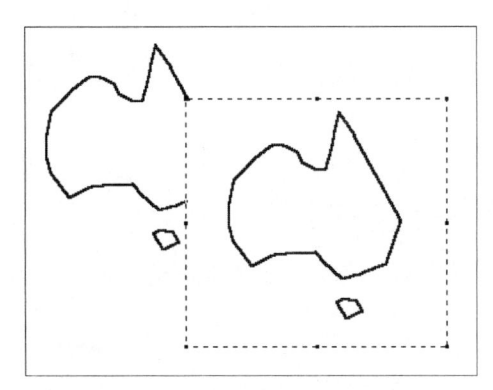

*The copy can be resized without any effect on the original drawing.*

Windows 98

PAINT

## Copying part of an image into a new document

Select the part you wish to copy.

**Edit - Copy To**

> Select the folder in the **Save in** list.
> Enter the name of the destination document in the **File Name** box.
> Click **Save**.

## Copying the content of a document into the Paint window

**Edit - Paste From**

> Open the folder containing the source document and double-click its name.
> In the option box, choose between a transparent or opaque copy.
> Once the image is in the Paint window, drag it into the correct place.
> Deselect the image by clicking outside it.

Windows 98

# Editing a drawing

## Copying part of an image into a new document

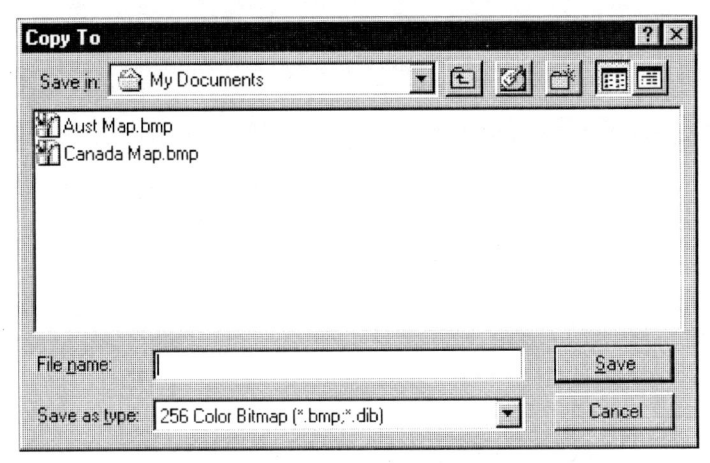

*Paint documents take a .bmp (bitmap) extension.*

## Copying the content of a document into the Paint window

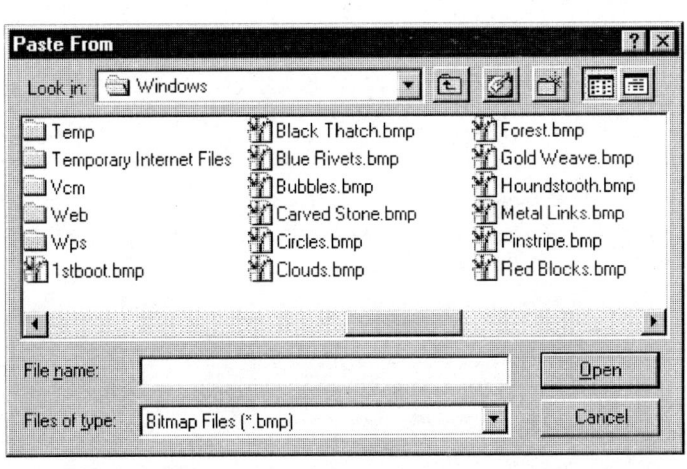

*Notice that by default the file type is bitmap.*

Windows 98

# PAINT

## Painting an area

Click in the color box to choose the colours you wish to use.

Select the [icon] tool.

Position the pointer in the image area so that the "paint" will pour from the pot onto the area you want to colour.

Left-click to paint with the foreground colour, or right-click to use the background colour.

*The area will be painted with the selected colour.*

Use **Edit - Undo** to undo the action.

> The same tool can be used to change the colour of a line.

## Creating a custom colour

Double-click any colour in the color box or use the **Colors - Edit Colors** command.

If you wish you can select a base colour which you can modify to create a custom colour then click **Define Custom Colors**.

> Choose a colour and click it, then use the slider to increase or decrease the luminosity of the colour to your taste.

You can also type in your own values for the **Hue**, **Sat** (saturation), **Lum** (luminosity) and the amount of **Red**, **Green** and **Blue**.

Click **Add to Custom Colors**.

*The colour appears under Custom colors.*

Click **OK**.

*The colour appears in the color box in the Paint window.*

A custom colour must be inserted into the active color box before it can be used (cf. Managing colours).

Windows 98

# Editing a drawing

## Painting an area

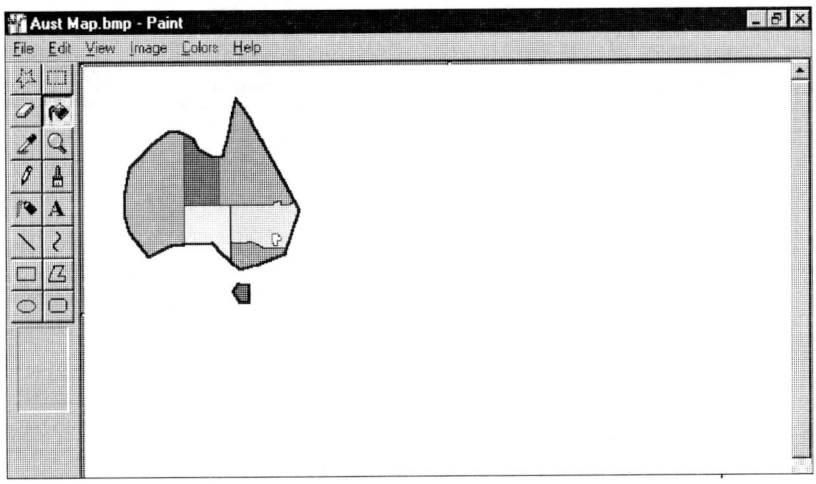

*If the area you are painting is not closed, the paint will run into adjacent areas.*

## Creating a custom colour

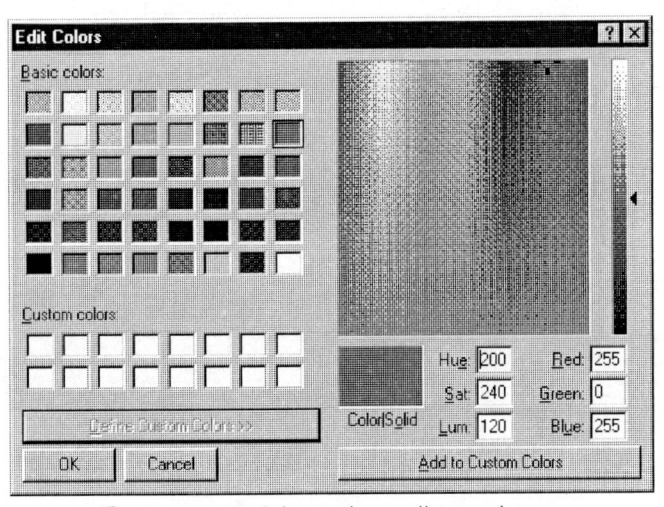

*The luminosity slider is the small triangle next to the luminosity bar.*

Windows 98

87

# PAINT

## Managing colours

**To make changes to the color box**, double-click the colour that you want to replace with another colour.

> Click the custom colour that will take its place or otherwise use the **Define Custom Colors** button to create a new colour.
> Click **OK**.

> To replace a color box colour by one of the colours displayed in the drawing, click the colour in the box, select the ![icon] tool then click the colour you wish to insert in its place.

## Wallpapering the Desktop

The background picture on the Desktop (wallpaper) is defined in the *Desktop* properties but can also be created in Paint.

Open or create the document containing the image you want to use as wallpaper.

Depending on how you want to arrange the image on the Desktop, choose from the **File** menu: **Set As Wallpaper (Tiled)** for a repeated image or **Set As Wallpaper (Centred)** for one central image.

Windows 98

# Editing a drawing

## Managing colours

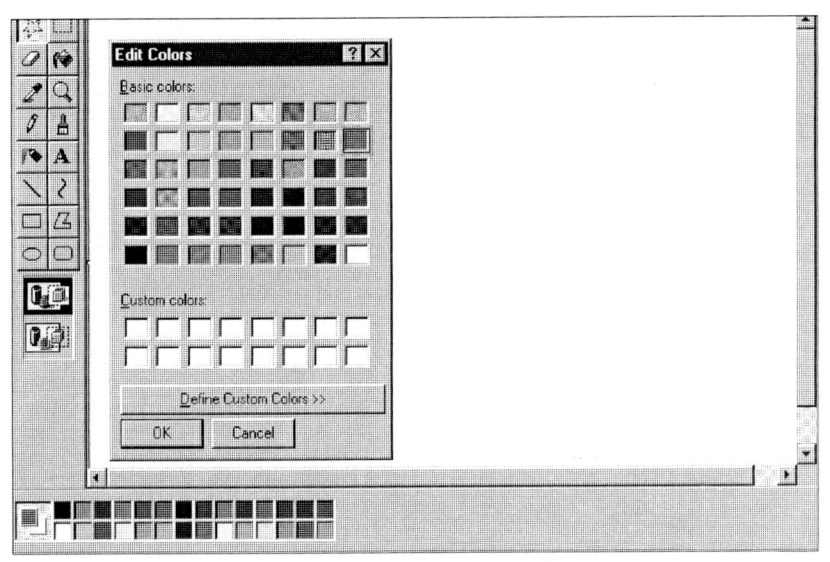

*The new colour replaces the previous one on the color box.*

## Wallpapering the Desktop

PAINT

## Zooming in on an image

*Magnifying the image on the screen helps you to be more precise when drawing details.*

Click [🔍].

*The mouse pointer appears as a magnifying glass inside a rectangle.*
*The option box allows you to select the scale of magnification (from X1 to X8).*

Move the pointer-rectangle so it encloses the part of the image you wish to zoom.

Click.

*The drawing is shown as a series of points. You can scroll the screen using the scroll bars and cursors.*

👆 Click the [🔍] tool again.

*The current magnification level can be seen in the option box.*
To return to a normal display, click the **1x** option or use [Ctrl] [Pg Up].

🔑 You can also activate the zoom by using **View - Zoom - Custom** then choose the required zoom level (from 100% to 800%).

## Working in Zoom mode

Click [🔍] to zoom the zone in which you want to work.

**To show the grid**, use the **View - Zoom - Show Grid** or [Ctrl] **G**.

*This grid helps you change artwork as you can see the position of the dots of colour very precisely. Each dot corresponds to a pixel.*

Select the appropriate tool for the changes you wish to make.

The [A] *tool is not available when you are in Zoom mode.*

Make any changes as you would in a normal screen mode. To draw new dots using the [✏️] tool, point to the corresponding square on the grid, then left-click to insert a dot in the foreground colour and right-click to make a dot in the background colour.

# Editing a drawing

## Zooming in on an image

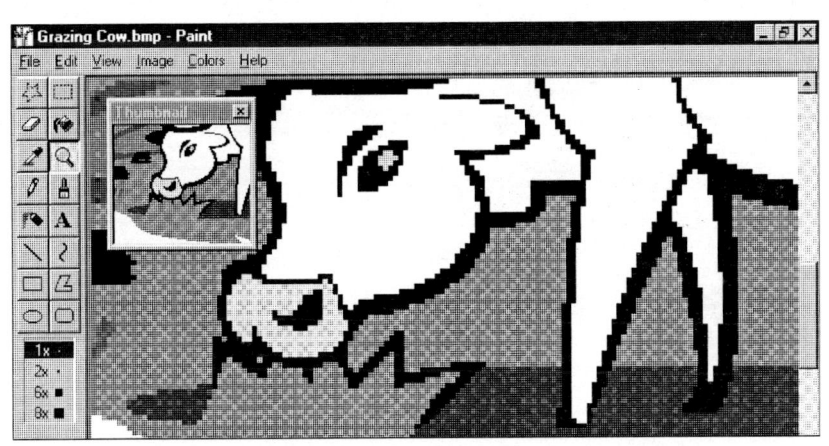

*The **Thumbnail** window contains a real-size picture of the image you have zoomed. It will appear if the **Show Thumbnail** option is active in the **View - Zoom** menu.*

## Working in Zoom mode

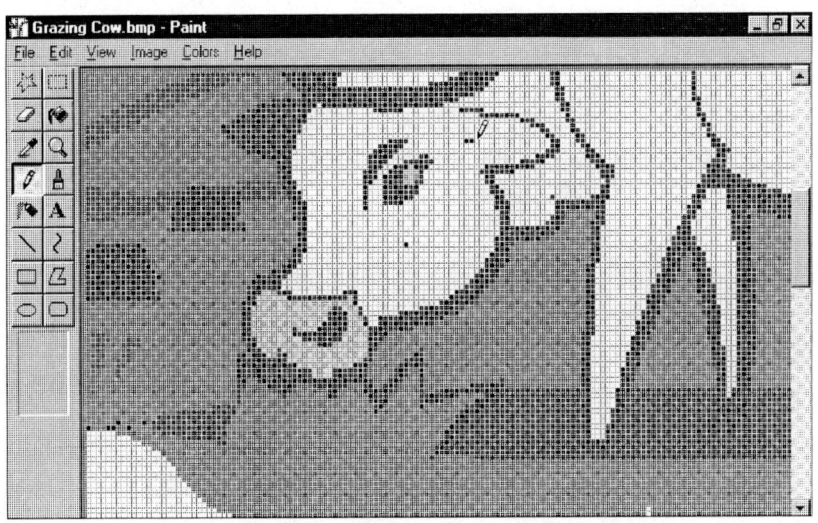

*In Zoom mode, you can insert dots along a straight line by holding down Shift as you drag the mouse.*

Windows 98

PAINT

## Resizing an image 🖱

Select the drawing concerned.

Point to one of the selection handles.
*The pointer takes the form of a two-headed arrow.*

> Drag the handle to enlarge or reduce the size of the image.

## Resizing an image

Select the drawing.
*If you forget to select, the size of the image area will be changed.*

**Image - Stretch/Skew** or [Ctrl] **W**

> Under **Stretch**, enter a percentage in the **Horizontal** text box to modify the image's width.
>
> Enter a percentage in the **Vertical** text box to change the image's height if required.
>
> Click **OK**.

Editing a drawing

## Resizing an image

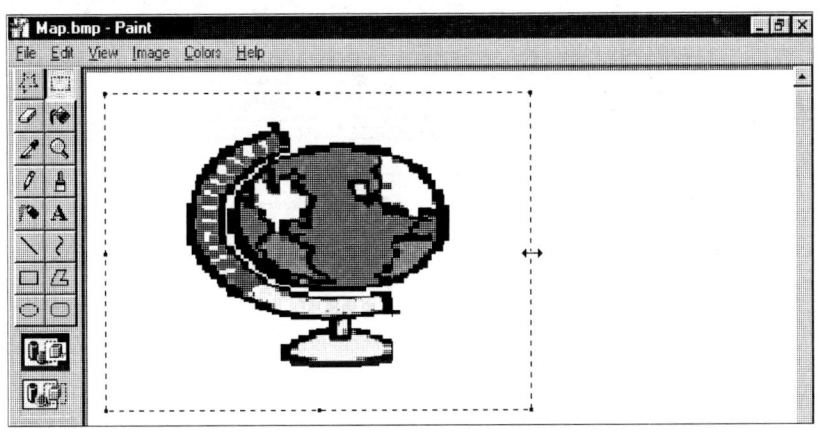

*This technique does not guarantee that the proportions of the drawing will not be changed.*

## Resizing an image

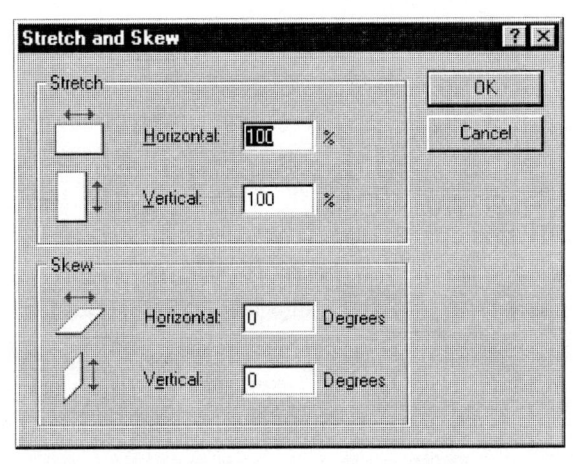

*By entering the same stretch percentages for the width and the height, the correct proportions for the drawing will be preserved.*

Windows 98

PAINT

## Skewing an image

Select the drawing.

**Image - Stretch/Skew** or [Ctrl] **W**

> Under **Skew**, click the **Horizontal** or **Vertical** text box, depending on the effect you had in mind.
> Specify the angle in degrees.
> Click **OK**.

## Rotating an image

Select the drawing, choosing an opaque or transparent selection.

**Image - Flip/Rotate** or [Ctrl] **R**

> Select one of these options:
> 
> | | |
> |---|---|
> | **Flip horizontal** | for a 180° rotation around a vertical axis. |
> | **Flip vertical** | for a 180° rotation around a horizontal axis. |
> | **Rotate by angle** | to rotate the selection through a selected angle. |
> 
> Click **OK**.
> 
> *This effect can be applied to the entire image area.*

# Editing a drawing

## Skewing an image

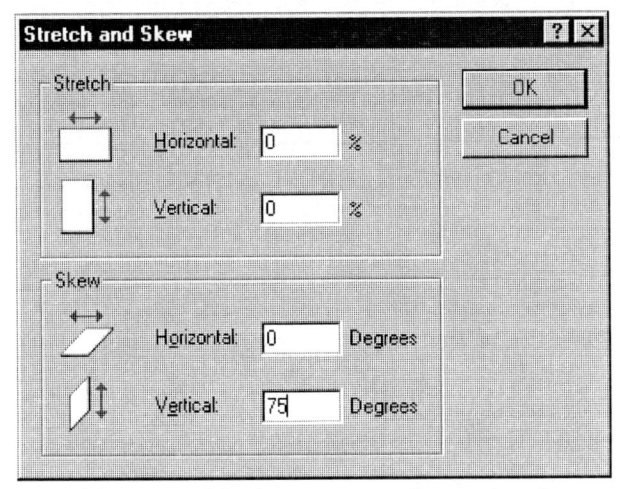

*You can modify the proportion of stretch and the skew angles simultaneously.*

## Rotating an image

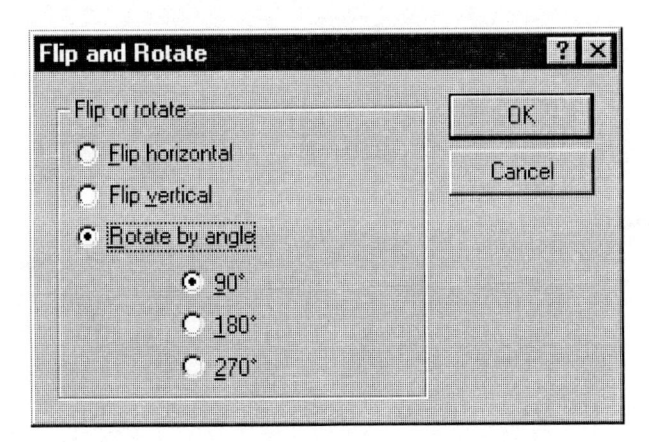

Windows 98

# PAINT

## YOUR NOTES

# Chapter 4

## EXPLORER

- **VIEWING DISK CONTENTS**    p.98
- **FOLDERS AND DOCUMENTS**    p.106

# EXPLORER

## Looking at the Explorer window

To start the Explorer, right-click the **My Computer** icon on the desktop and choose **Explore**, or click the **Start** button, point to the **Programs** option and click **Windows Explorer**.

*The Explorer window appears.*

Apart from the elements which are common to all windows, the Explorer window contains:

- The **Standard Buttons** bar (a): the first two buttons on this bar allow you to move from one window to another as if you were browsing the Web.
- The **Address** bar (b) displays the path of access to the selected folder. The path is a series of folders and subfolders that you must open to reach the current folder. Click the ▼ button to open the list and access all the levels of the Desktop hierarchy. You can also enter a path or an Internet address directly into the text box.
- Two panes separated by a **split bar** (c).
- The left pane, or **Explorer bar** (d) contains the set of objects existing on the Desktop: **My Computer, My Documents** folder, **Network Neighborhood, Recycle Bin, Online Services** folder. You can change the contents of the left pane using **View - Explorer Bar**, or remove it from the window.
- The right pane (e), contains a list of what is contained in the item highlighted in the left pane (documents or folders).

*The contents of these two panes can vary, depending on the activated viewing options.*

**To display or hide the toolbar and/or status bar**, activate or deactivate the corresponding options in the **View** menu.

*The drop-down list on the toolbar lets you quickly access the different items on the Desktop.*

**To change the width of each pane**, point to the split bar and drag left or right.

# Viewing disk contents

## Looking at the Explorer window

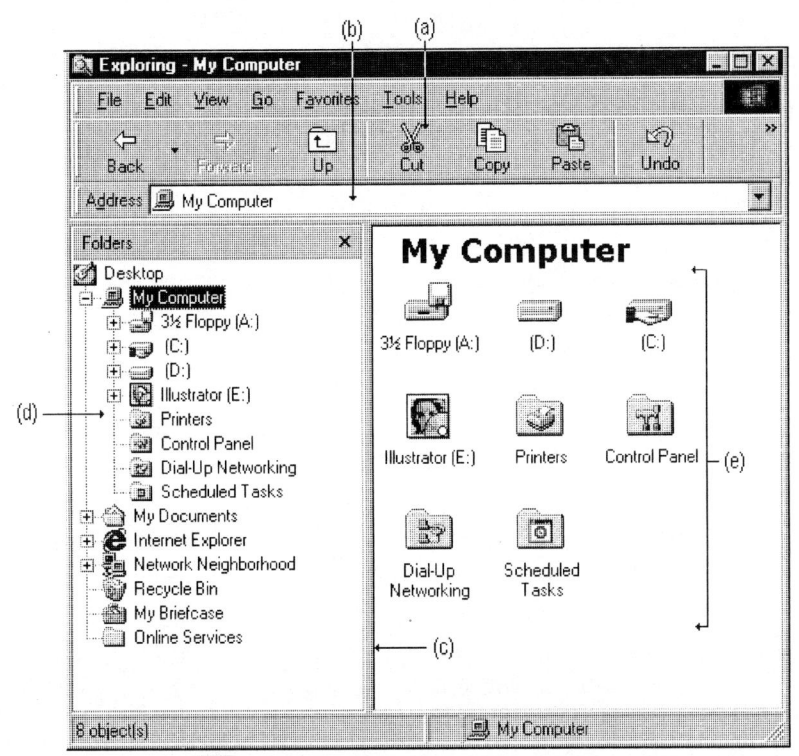

The [F6] key can be used to switch from one pane to another and to the address bar.

Windows 98

# EXPLORER

## Managing views of the Explorer

**To close the Explorer bar**, click the ☒ button on the top right of the bar.

*Only the right pane remains in the window: the name of the folder whose contents you are seeing appears in the Address bar.*

**To restore the Explorer bar**, open the View menu then **Explorer Bar**.

➥ Click the option which corresponds to what you want to see in the Explorer bar. The first four options are also available in the Internet Explorer: they allow you to access Web pages. To display the full hierarchical tree of your disk, choose **All Folders**.

**To display the Explorer as a Web page**, open the View menu and choose as **Web Page**.

*The as Web Page view shows the document's properties in the pane on the right. If the selected document is a bitmap, a preview of the image also appears.*

**To show or hide the status bar**, open the View menu and activate or deactivate the **Status Bar** option.

*The status bar shows various information concerning the selected object(s).*

**To show or hide a toolbar**, use View - Toolbar and activate or deactivate the option which corresponds to the toolbar you want to show (or hide).

*The Links bar provides rapid access to certain Internet sites.*

100     Windows 98

# Viewing disk contents

## Managing views of the Explorer

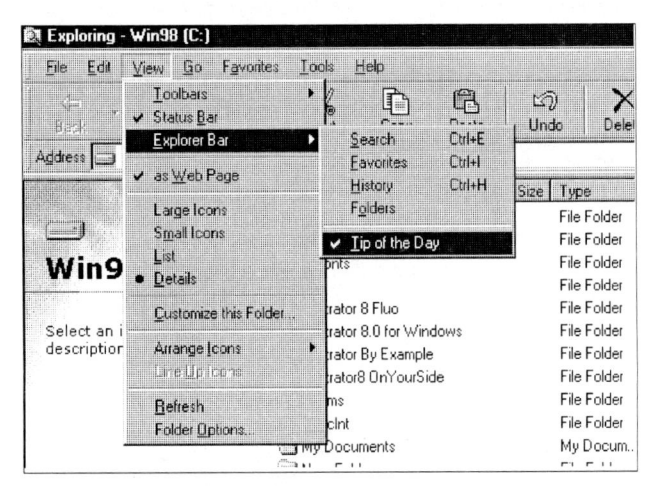

*Click **Tip of the Day** to open a new pane at the bottom of the screen containing a useful tip.*

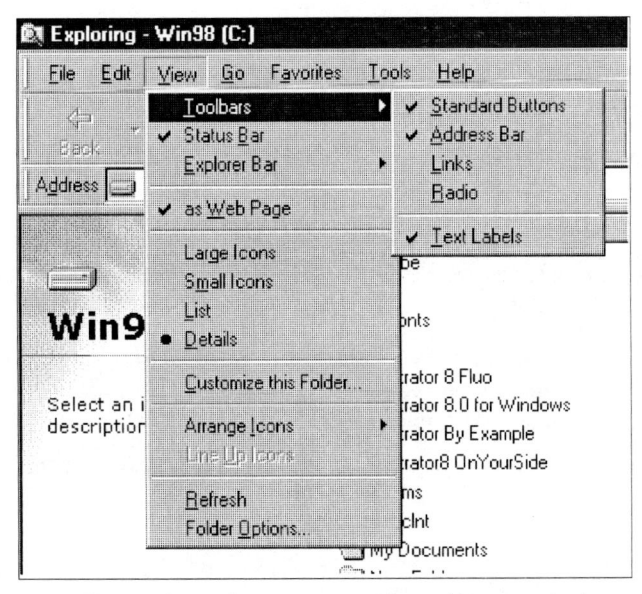

*The toolbars that are currently visible are ticked.*

Windows 98

# EXPLORER

## Going into a drive/a folder

The various Desktop items are presented in a tree hierarchy. Some branches of the tree are expanded (a), so that the folders and objects they contain are visible; others (b) are collapsed.

An expanded branch is marked with a - sign: a collapsed branch is marked by a + sign. To expand or collapse a branch, just click on the + or - sign.

*My Computer* contains 8 items in this example: the first four correspond to the computer's disk drives, although it is possible to have only three or occasionally more than four drives. There should be a floppy disk drive (A:), at least one hard disk (C:) and usually one CD-ROM drive (here, this is E:). Next there are four folders (note how each icon is different): the **Control Panel**, used to define the computer's configuration; the **Printers** folder, used for installing or managing a printer; the **Dial-Up Networking** folder, for connecting with a remote computer using a modem; the **Scheduled Tasks** folder, containing tasks that you have programmed to run at a set time in the **Task Scheduler**.

**To see the contents of a folder or item,** click it.

**To expand a branch completely,** click the branch and type *.

*When a folder is open, there is a change in the icon representing it.*

**To go the folder above** (the folder which contains the current folder), use **Go - Up One Level** or press ⬅.

**To go back to a previously-opened folder or drive,** use the **Go - Back** command or click the [Back] button on the **Standard Buttons** toolbar or press [Alt]⬅.

**To display the next page,** use the **Go - Forward** command or click the [Forward] button on the **Standard Buttons** toolbar or press [Alt]➡.

**To display any previously opened page,** open the [Back] or [Forward] list and click the name of the page you want to display.

*When a folder appears in the right pane, double-click its icon (not its name) to display its contents.*

To update the data in one of the panes, use the **View - Refresh** command (or [F5]).

# Viewing disk contents

## Going into a drive/a folder

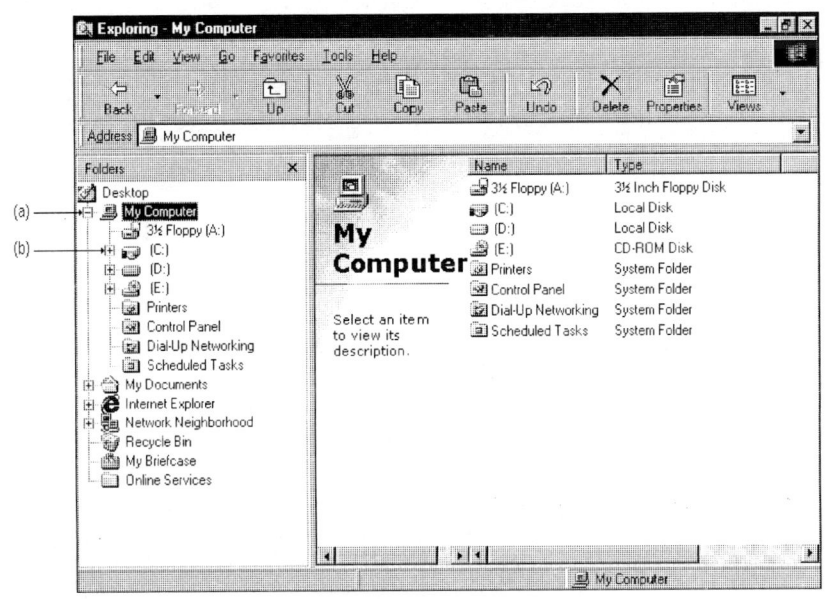

[Screenshot: Exploring - My Computer window showing folder tree on left with (a) pointing to My Computer and (b) pointing to the [+] expand icon next to C:. Right pane lists 3½ Floppy (A:), (C:), (D:), (E:), Printers, Control Panel, Dial-Up Networking, Scheduled Tasks with their types.]

*The right pane shows the contents of the selected item.*
*Here, **My Computer**.*

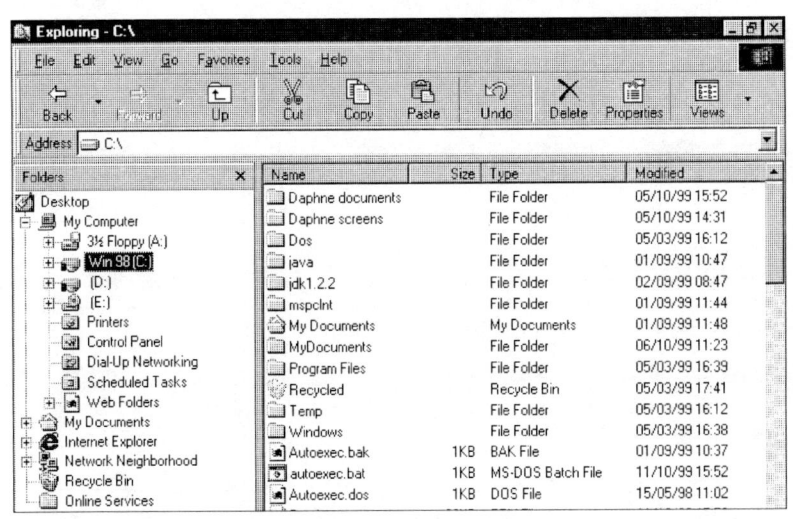

[Screenshot: Exploring - C:\ window. Folders pane shows Desktop > My Computer > 3½ Floppy (A:), Win 98 (C:), (D:), (E:), Printers, Control Panel, Dial-Up Networking, Scheduled Tasks, Web Folders, My Documents, Internet Explorer, Network Neighborhood, Recycle Bin, Online Services. Right pane lists files:]

| Name | Size | Type | Modified |
|---|---|---|---|
| Daphne documents | | File Folder | 05/10/99 15:52 |
| Daphne screens | | File Folder | 05/10/99 14:31 |
| Dos | | File Folder | 05/03/99 16:12 |
| java | | File Folder | 01/09/99 10:47 |
| jdk1.2.2 | | File Folder | 02/09/99 08:47 |
| mspcInt | | File Folder | 01/09/99 11:44 |
| My Documents | | My Documents | 01/09/99 11:48 |
| MyDocuments | | File Folder | 06/10/99 11:23 |
| Program Files | | File Folder | 05/03/99 16:39 |
| Recycled | | Recycle Bin | 05/03/99 17:41 |
| Temp | | File Folder | 05/03/99 16:12 |
| Windows | | File Folder | 05/03/99 16:38 |
| Autoexec.bak | 1KB | BAK File | 01/09/99 10:37 |
| autoexec.bat | 1KB | MS-DOS Batch File | 11/10/99 15:52 |
| Autoexec.dos | 1KB | DOS File | 15/05/98 11:02 |

*The right pane shows the contents of drive C:. The folders are listed first, in alphabetical order. In the file hierarchy, this branch has not been expanded.*

Windows 98                                                                 103

# EXPLORER

## Setting out the list of documents

*You can choose the items which make up the right pane and the options for viewing them.*

Open the **View** menu or click the arrow next to the **Views** button on the **Standard Buttons** bar to open its list.

*Clicking the* **Views** *button itself changes the way the list is presented; click once for large icons, twice for small icons, three times for a list and four times for a detailed list.*

Choose one of these viewing options:

**Large Icons/Small Icons** — to display the icon and the name of each document; there are no restrictions on the arrangement of the icons and you can move them around in the window.

**List** — to display a small icon and the name of each document; the icons form an alphabetically classified list and cannot be moved.

**Details** — to display the name and icon, but also the file's size, its type and the date and time it was last modified.

*The file size is expressed in* **Kilobytes (Kb)** *(a byte is equivalent to the space taken up by one character).*

*A file's type is linked to its format. Windows 98 recognises most file formats. However, if this is not the case, XXX file (where XXX is the extension) appears in the type column.*

*The date and time of the last modification are calculated using the control date and time of your computer (which contains an internal clock).*

## Sorting the list of documents

**View - Arrange Icons**

Activate the option for the sort order you prefer.

*When documents appear as a detailed list, you can sort the list according to the contents of a particular column by clicking the column heading. It is sorted in ascending order; click again to sort it in descending order.*

# Viewing disk contents

## Setting out the list of documents

*Each icon represents a different type of file. When in **Large Icon** mode, you can drag the icons to move them around in the window.*

## Sorting the list of documents

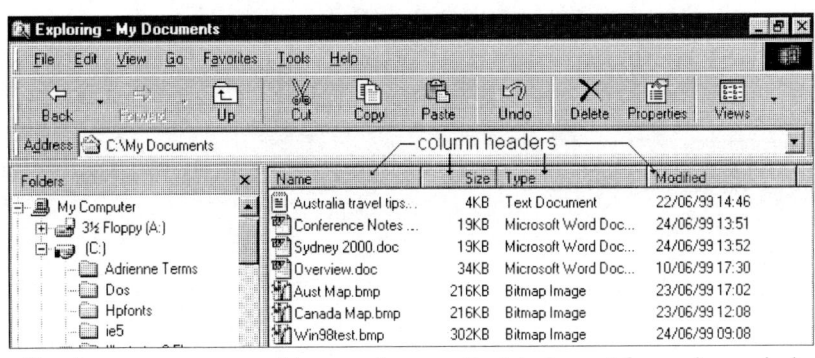

*The documents are sorted by size, from smallest to largest (ascending order).*

Windows 98

EXPLORER

## Selecting documents (double-click setting)

Point to a space to the right of the first document to select and drag to enclose all the required names and icons in a dotted rectangle.

*However, if your pointer suddenly appears as a circle with a line through it (a no-go sign) and the files move as you drag, let go of the button at once.*

*The number of documents selected can be seen on the status bar as well as their combined size.*

**To spread the selection to adjacent documents**, hold down [Shift] and click the last document to include in the selection.

**To select an additional group of documents**, hold down [Shift] and drag round the new group.

**To add a document into the selection**, hold down [Ctrl] and click the document.

**To select all documents**, use **Edit - Select All** or [Ctrl] **A**.

*You can invert the selection using the command in the Edit menu.*

You can also select using the keyboard: access the first document, hold down [Shift] and use the arrow keys to spread the selection. To select a document which is not adjacent to the first ones selected, hold down [Ctrl] while pressing [↑] or [↓] to reach the document then press [space] to select it.

*When a selection has been made, right-click it to see its shortcut menu (a menu containing only options relevant to the selected object).*

## Deselecting documents (double-click setting)

**To deselect certain documents**, hold down [Ctrl] and drag around the documents to be deselected.

**To deselect all the documents**, click anywhere else in the window (avoid clicking the name of any document).

# Folders and documents

## Selecting documents (double-click setting)

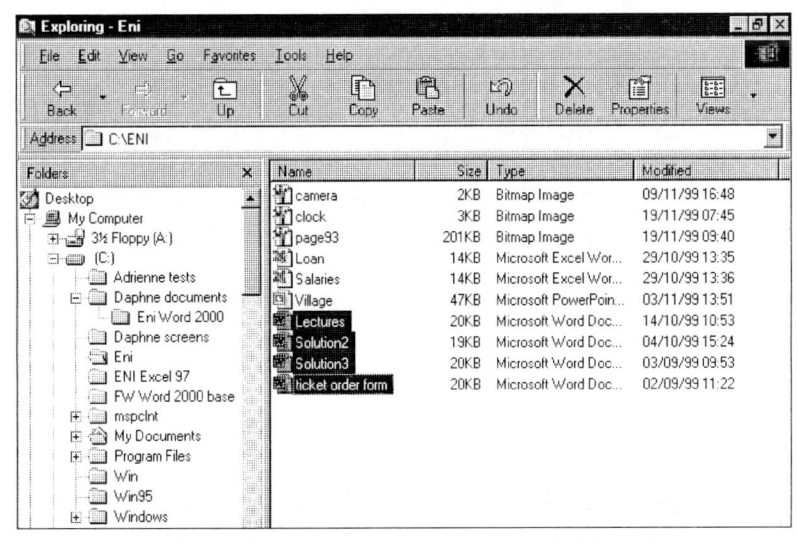

*The selected names have been colour-highlighted.*

## Deselecting documents (double-click setting)

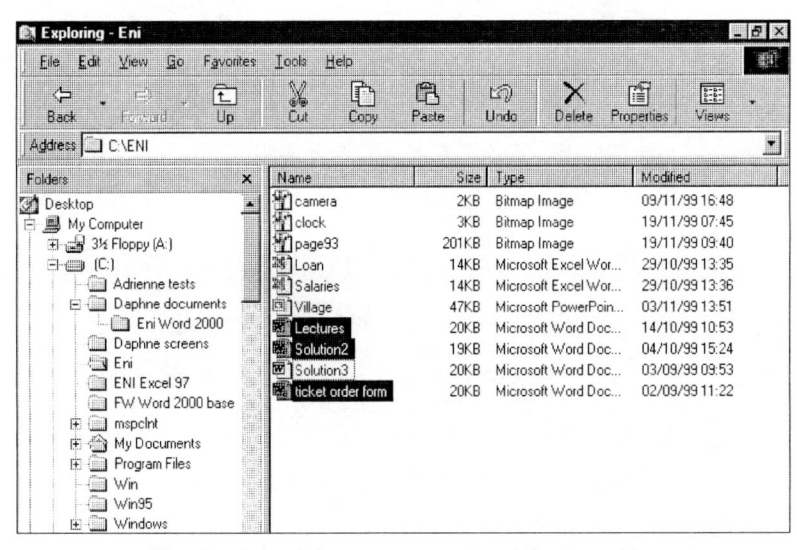

*The deselected document is enclosed by dotted lines.*

EXPLORER

## Searching for one or more documents by name

Tools - Find - Files or Folders

☞ Check the **Name & Location** tab is selected.

In the drop-down list called **Named**, specify the name of the document to find. If you are looking for more than one document, or you are unsure of the name, you can use the wildcard characters * and ?:

*     to represent a string of characters of varying length

?     to represent a single character

If you know a part of the text contained within the document, you can enter this in the **Containing text** box.

Use the **Look in** list to choose the drive or folder in which to search or click the **Browse** button to select it in the hierarchy.

Deactivate the **Include subfolders** option if you only want to search in the active folder.

If Windows has to look for the name exactly as you have typed it (with the same combination of capitals and lower case letters), activate the **Case Sensitive** option in the **Options** menu.

Click the **Find Now** button to start searching.

*The search result, that is all of the documents which correspond to your search criteria, appears in the lower part of the window.*

☞ To maximize this new window to full screen size, click the 🔲 button.

*You can modify the column widths as with any list.*

To change the way in which the list is presented, use one of the first four options on the **View** menu.

To clear the list of documents and cancel the current search criteria (in any tab), click the **New Search** button.

*The lower part of the window disappears.*

108         Windows 98

# Folders and documents

## Searching for one or more documents by name

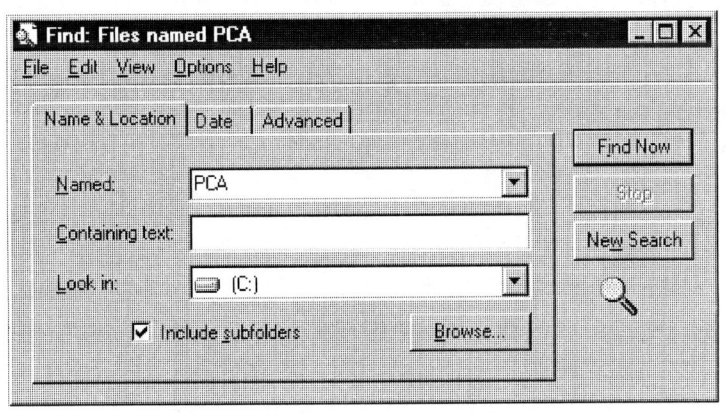

*Opening the Named drop-down list shows a list of criteria used for previous searches, which you can select if you wish.*

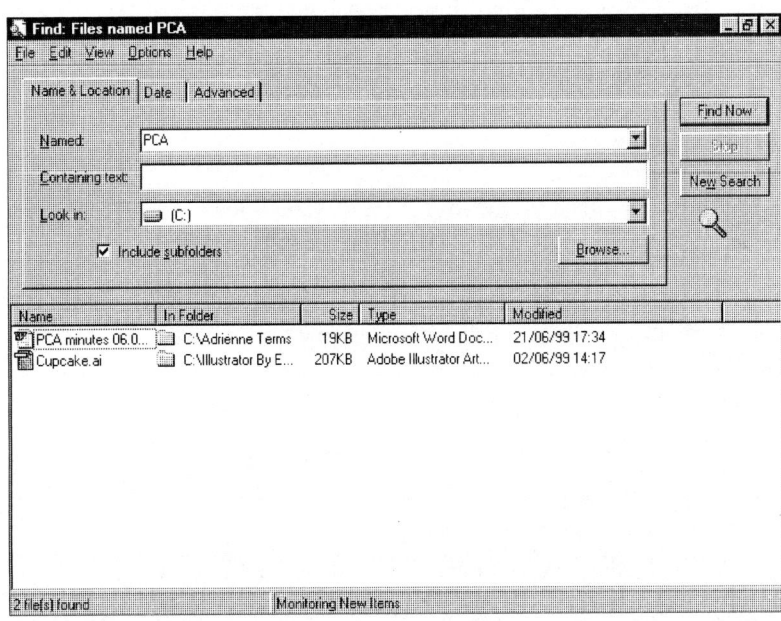

*This search found all the items containing "PCA" in the title (notice that the result is a little surprising, as the Case Sensitive option was not used). The number of files located can be seen on the status bar.*

Windows 98

# EXPLORER

## Searching for one or more documents by modification date

In the **Find** window (**Tools - Find - Files or Folders**), check the options on the **Name & Location** tab.

Click the **Date** tab.

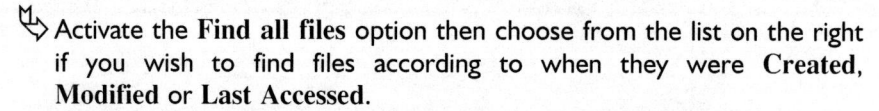

> Activate the **Find all files** option then choose from the list on the right if you wish to find files according to when they were **Created**, **Modified** or **Last Accessed**.
>
> Use the next options to define the time period involved (an interval between two dates or a number of months/days previous to the current date).
>
> Click the **Find Now** button.

> The **File - Save Search** command will let you create a shortcut on the Desktop to access the list of documents corresponding to the search criteria quickly.

## Creating a folder

Select the folder inside which you want to create a new folder.

**File - New - Folder**

*You can also right-click an empty space in the list and choose New then Folder.*
*A new folder icon appears: this folder is temporarily named New Folder. The name is highlighted and the insertion point flashes at the end of the name, which means you can name the folder yourself.*

> Enter the new folder's name. This name can contain up to 255 characters, including spaces, but you cannot use the characters \ ? : * " or |. You can however use capital letters.
>
> Confirm by pressing [Enter].
>
> *The new folder is empty for now.*
> *In the Explorer bar, the folder above the new folder shows a + sign because it now contains a subfolder.*
>
> *When document lists are sorted in ascending order, folder names automatically appear at the head of the list.*

110                                                                 Windows 98

# Folders and documents

## Searching for one or more documents by modification date

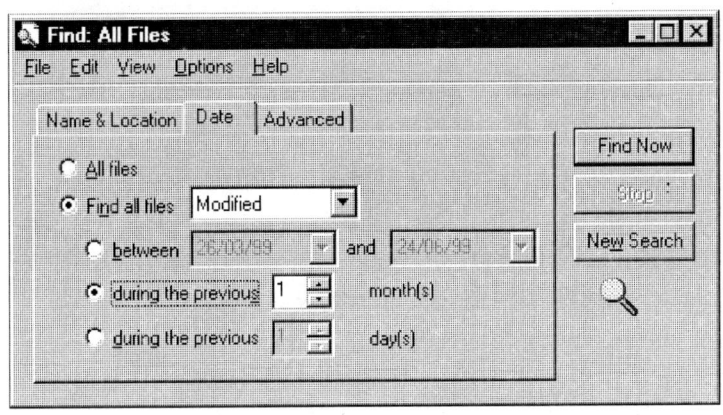

*This search will look for all documents modified during the last month.*

## Creating a folder

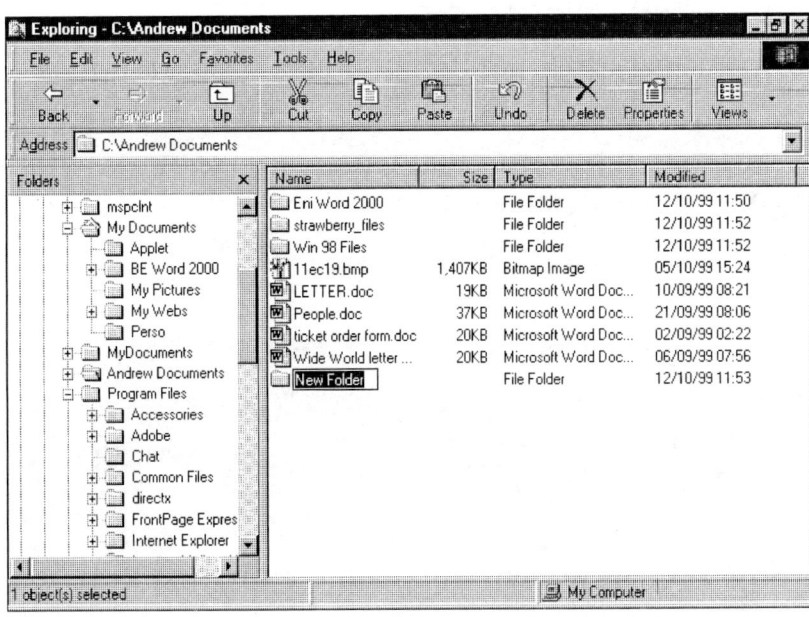

*Notice that, like the other folders, the new folder does not have a size.*

Windows 98

# EXPLORER

## Copying folders or documents using the clipboard

Select the folder or the documents.

Copy them onto the clipboard using **Edit - Copy** or [Copy] or [Ctrl] **C**.

Select the folder into which you want to copy the folder or documents.

Paste in the contents of the clipboard using **Edit - Paste** or [Paste] or [Ctrl] **V**.

*The documents appear in the right pane. They are still in the clipboard, and you can copy them into another folder if you wish.*

*When you copy a folder, you copy its whole file hierarchy, that is any folders it may contain and also all the documents contained in these subfolders.*

*If the folder into which you are copying already contains a document of the same name, Windows will want to overwrite (or replace) it with the one you are pasting in! But it will ask you for confirmation before doing so.*

*If you copy a document into its original folder, Windows creates a duplicate of it, called Copy of... followed by the document's name.*

*If you copy onto a network drive which will not accept long file names, you will have to confirm that the first eight characters of the name can be used as the name of the destination document.*

## Copying folders or documents

Select the folder or document you want to copy.

Make sure the destination folder can be seen in the file hierarchy (if it is part of another folder, this one must be open).

Drag the folder or document onto the destination folder: hold down [Ctrl] if you are copying onto the same disk drive.

*While you drag, a + sign will accompany the pointer on the screen.*

You can also make a copy by dragging with the right mouse button. When you arrive at the destination folder, click **Copy here** in the shortcut menu which appears.

Windows 98

# Folders and documents

## Copying folders or documents using the clipboard

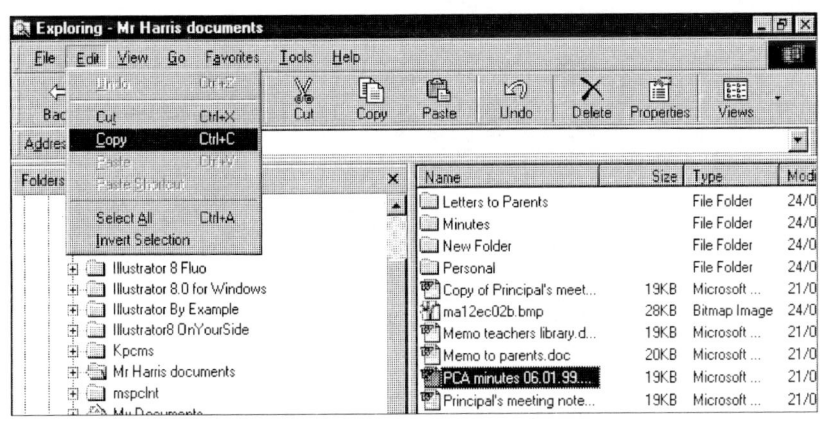

*The **Paste** option is only available in the menu once you have chosen to Copy something.*

## Copying folders or documents

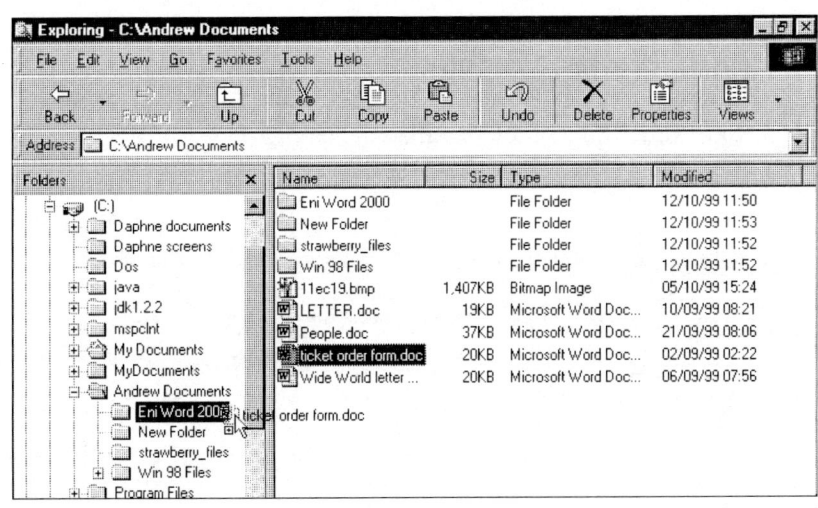

*When copying, make sure that the destination folder in the left pane is selected (colour-highlighted) before releasing the mouse.*

Windows 98

113

# EXPLORER

## Copying folders or documents onto a diskette

Make sure the diskette in the floppy disk drive has been formatted.

Select the folders or documents concerned.

Right-click to show the shortcut menu for the selected items.

> Point to the **Send to** option then click the name corresponding to the floppy disk drive for example, **Floppy disk (A:)**.
>
> A *Copying...* window shows how the copy is progressing. You will probably also hear the disk drive turning over and see a light next to your disk which will indicate that a copy is in progress.

## Renaming a folder or document

Select the document or folder to be renamed.

Click the name, at the place you wish to put the insertion point or use the **File - Rename** command.

*The name is no longer selected when the coloured highlighting has disappeared.*

> Use the usual keys to move around in and edit the text.
>
> Remember that the keys \ ? : * " | cannot be used.
>
> Confirm.
>
> *The name is automatically modified. If the active folder contains a document of the same name, Windows will ask if you wish to replace the document by the renamed folder.*

# Folders and documents

## Copying folders or documents onto a diskette

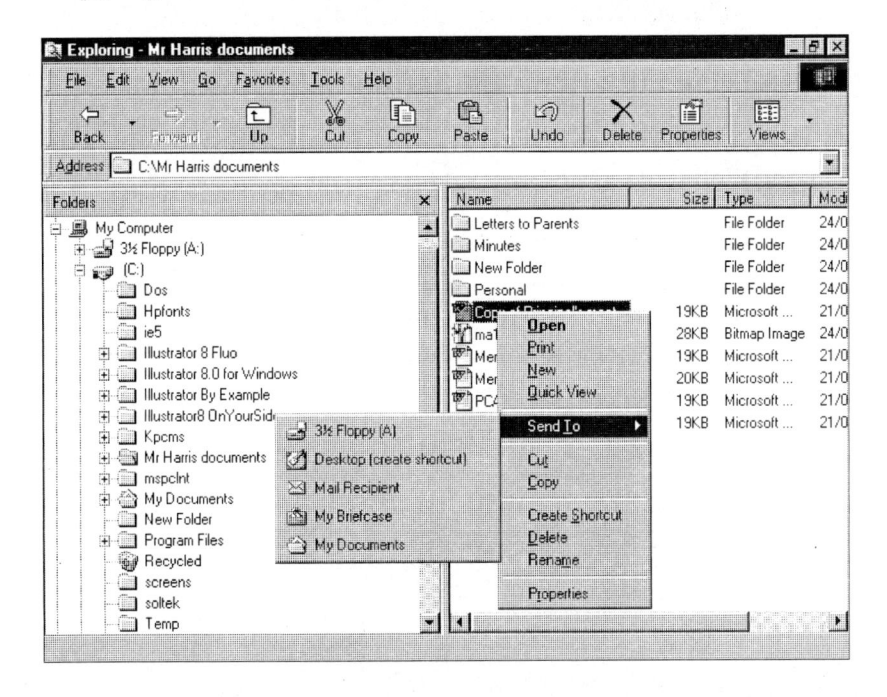

## Renaming a folder or document

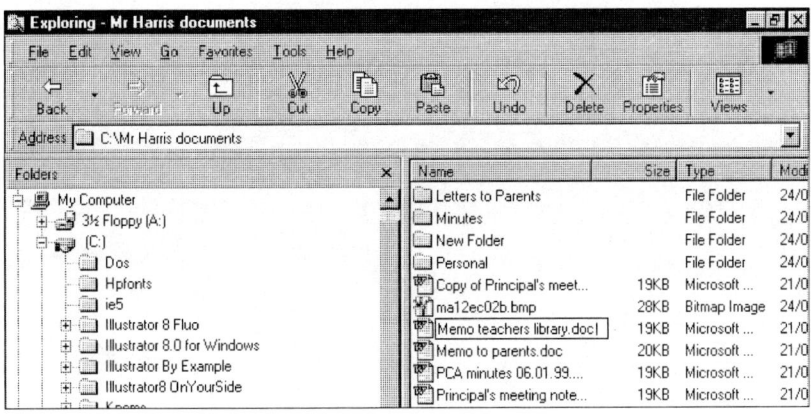

*The flashing insertion point indicates that you can start editing the name.*

Windows 98

EXPLORER

## Moving a folder or documents using the clipboard

Select the folder or documents you wish to move.

*You cannot select more than one folder in the Explorer bar.*

Place the objects onto the clipboard using **Edit - Cut** or [Cut] or [Ctrl] **X**.

☞ Select the destination folder.

Paste in the contents of the clipboard using **Edit - Paste** or [Paste] or [Ctrl] **V**.

*There is a very short delay, then you will see the cut document appear in the folder you have selected.*

## Moving a folder or documents

Select the folder or documents concerned.

Drag the selection. Hold down [⇧ Shift] as you drag if you are moving it into another drive.

*When you point at the destination folder, a + sign must not appear near the pointer.*

*When you have finished, the items should no longer be visible in the open folder.*

🔑 You can also right-click then drag to the destination folder. Choose **Move Here** in the shortcut menu.

# Folders and documents

## Moving a folder or documents using the clipboard

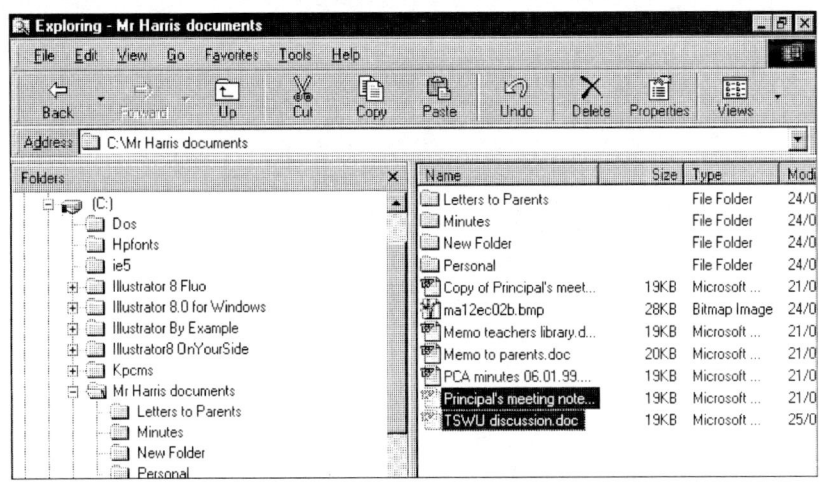

*After you have chosen **Cut**, the document names are still visible, but the icons representing them have become semitransparent.*

## Moving a folder or documents

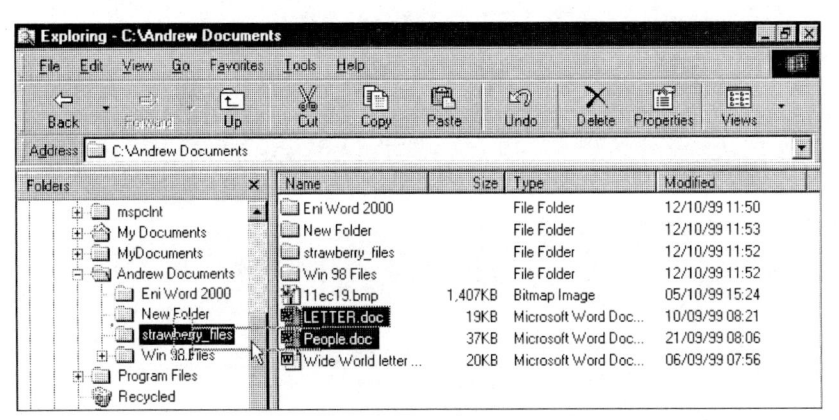

*Before releasing the mouse, make sure you have selected the correct destination folder.*

Windows 98 117

EXPLORER

## Deleting a folder or documents

Select the folder or documents you wish to delete.

**File - Delete** or press [Del] or click [Delete].

  👆 Click **Yes** to confirm deletion and send the documents or folder to the Recycle Bin.

*The folder or documents quickly disappear from the file hierarchy.*

*Deleting a folder means deleting not only its documents but also any subfolders it may contain.*

*Deleting is not irreversible: the documents still physically exist on the hard disk, but are just not visible in the folders. But be careful, this only applies to your hard disk; deletions made on any other drive, such as the floppy disk drive or on another workstation, are permanent and cannot be reversed!*

*To permanently delete a document, thus creating extra space on the disk, you must remove items from the Recycle Bin or empty the bin.*

  🔑 To permanently delete an item, without passing by the Recycle Bin, you can use [⇧ Shift][Del], instead of just [Del].

## Opening an application from the Explorer

**To open an application from a program file or a document**, double-click the icon of the program file or document which has been created in the application. This will open it. You can also select the document name and press [Enter] or choose **Open** in the **File** menu.

*A program file has an extension COM, EXE...*

*Windows starts the application then opens the document.*

# Folders and documents

## Deleting a folder or documents

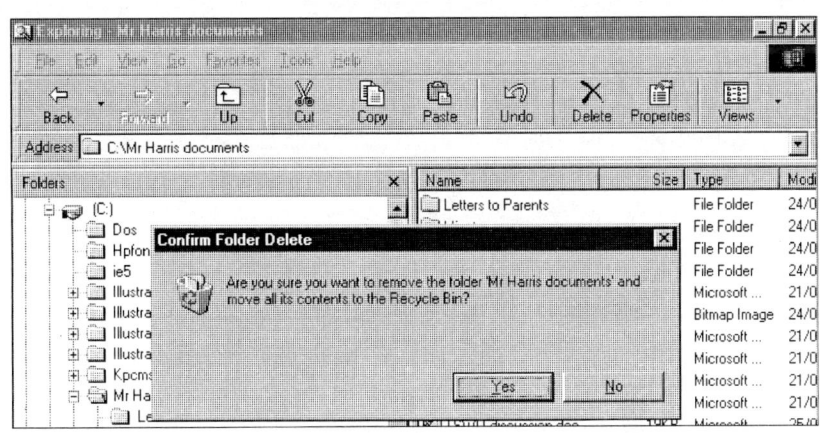

*You can choose not to display this request for confirmation when deleting by deactivating the **Display delete confirmation dialog box** option, which you can find by right-clicking the Recycle Bin icon, choosing **Properties**, then the **General** tab.*

## Opening an application from the Explorer

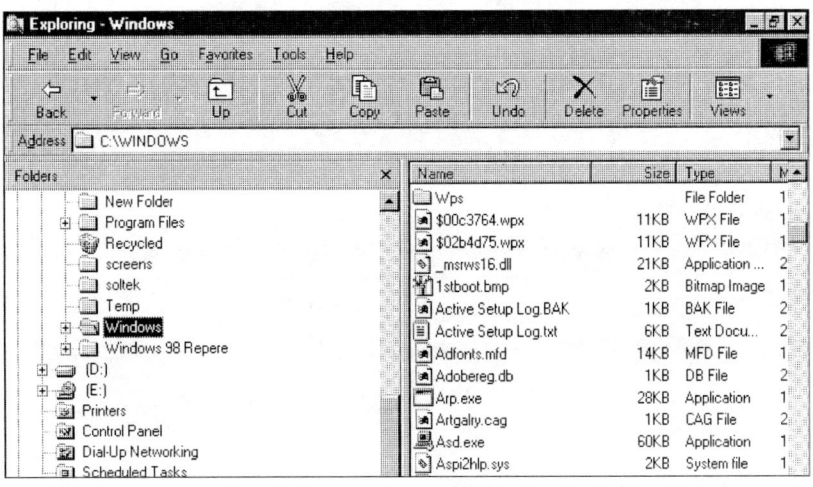

*Notice how each type of program or application has a specific icon.*

Windows 98

119

EXPLORER

## Managing folders/documents located in the Recycle Bin

**To display these documents**, double-click the **Recycle Bin** icon on the Desktop to open it.

*You can see the list of documents contained within the Recycle Bin. You can work with this list in the same way as the Explorer window. The* View *menu options allow you to change the way it is displayed. If the* as Web Page *view is activated, a description of the Recycle Bin folder appears in the left side of the window.*

➪ **To recover one, or several documents or folders**, select them in the Recycle Bin window.

**File - Restore**

*The folder or document will disappear from the Recycle Bin. It is available once again in the Explorer window. If necessary, Windows 98 will recreate the original folder which contained the document.*

**To delete one or more documents or folders permanently**, select them in the Recycle Bin window and use **File - Delete** or [Del].

**To empty the Recycle Bin**, choose **File - Empty Recycle Bin** in the Recycle Bin window. Click **Yes** to confirm deletion of all the items contained in the bin.

*The Recycle Bin is now empty again, until you transfer other items into it.*

🔑 You can also right-click the **Recycle Bin** icon and choose **Empty Recycle Bin**.

## Printing a document from the Explorer

Select the documents concerned, then choose **File - Print**.

*You can also right-click the selection and choose* **Print**.
*The documents are sent to the Print Manager; the printer icon appears on the Taskbar.*

🔑 If the printer icon is present on the Desktop, you can drag the selection onto the icon.

# Folders and documents

## Managing folders/documents located in the Recycle Bin

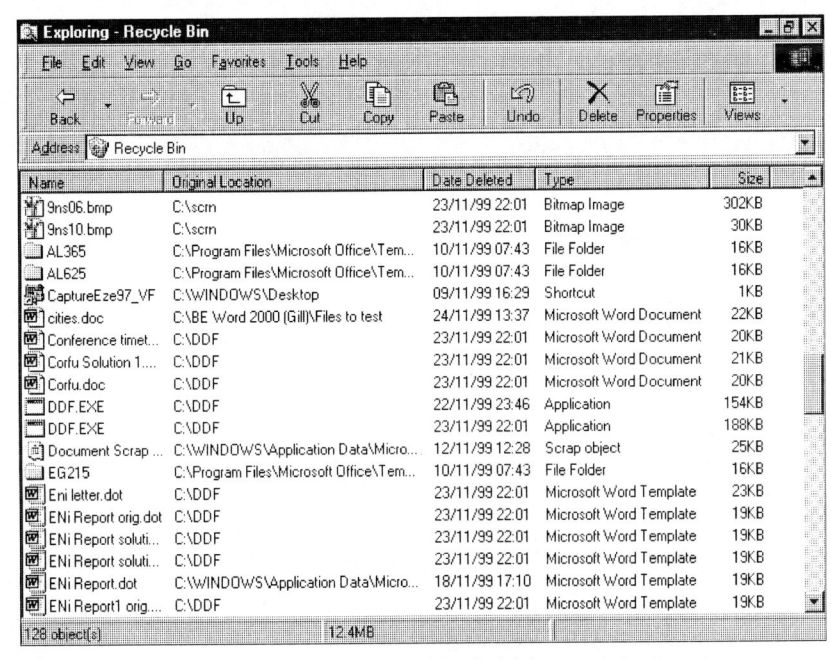

*Notice that the list contains both folders and documents.*

## Printing a document from the Explorer

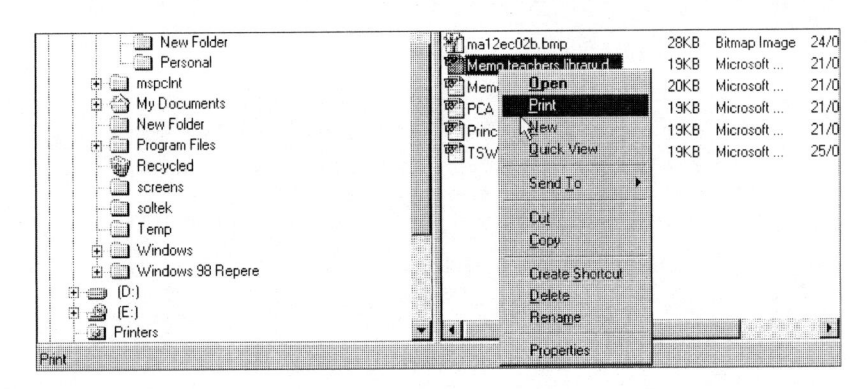

Windows 98

# EXPLORER

## Sharing a folder with network users

*If you work as part of a network, you can access shared folders on other workstations on your network. In the same way, if another user is to access some or all of your documents, you must share them to allow access.*

Right-click the folder or drive that you wish to share then click the **Sharing...** option.

 Activate the **Shared as** option.
Specify the name of the folder. This name will be shown on the other workstations when they access your computer.
In the next text box, you can add a comment for other users if you wish.
Specify the type of access you wish to allow;

**Read-Only**   network users can read the contents of your folder and start the application it uses, but they cannot write in it (they cannot edit, delete or move a document for example).

**Full**   gives other users full access to the folders, subfolders and documents specified, including the possibility of editing or deleting them (but you may ask for a password).

**Depends on Password**   Other users will have to supply the correct password to display the folder contents and/or perform any tasks concerning them.

You can enter different passwords for read-only and full access if you wish, then click **OK**. Type the password(s) again to confirm.

*The folder icon has changed and now looks like this:* .
*Any sub-folders in the folder are also accessible.*

**To check that the folder has been correctly shared**, you need to go to another workstation on your network. If this one is using Windows 98, open the Network Neighborhood folder (in the Explorer or on the Desktop) to access the shared folder.

**To cancel sharing a folder or drive**, right-click the item, choose **Sharing...** activate the **Not shared** option and click **OK**.

*If any other users are connected to your workstation, the connection will be broken.*

In this case, click **Yes** to confirm.

# Folders and documents

## Sharing a folder with network users

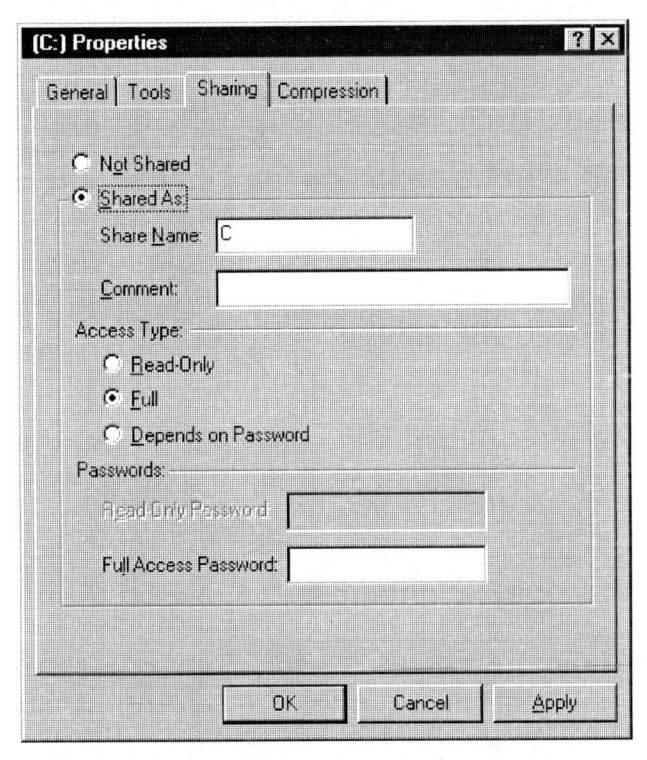

*The **Apply** button allows you to apply the parameters you have just defined without closing the dialog box.*

Windows 98

# EXPLORER

## YOUR NOTES

# Chapter 5
## MULTIMEDIA

- **CD PLAYER** p.126
- **MEDIA PLAYER** p.130
- **SOUND RECORDER** p.132

MULTIMEDIA

## Listening to an audio CD

Insert any audio CD into your computer's CD-ROM drive then start the **CD Player** application found in **Programs - Accessories - Entertainment**.

If necessary, display the toolbar using **View - Toolbar**.

➤ **To play a track on your CD**, open the **Track** list box and click ▶. Move from track to track using the CD Player buttons:

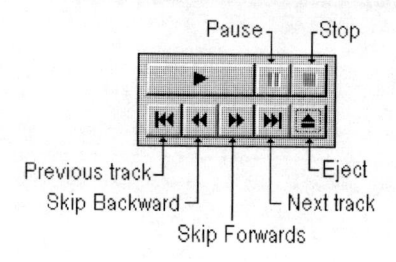

```
              Pause   ┌Stop
                ▶  ║  ■
           ◄◄ ◄ ► ►► ▲
Previous track─┘ │ │  └Eject
   Skip Backward─┘ │  └ Next track
          Skip Forwards
```

The number of the track being played will be displayed, as well as its length in minutes.

The CD may play automatically on insertion provided the **Auto insert notification** option is active (you can find this option by the rather tortuous path of: **Start - Settings - Control Panel - System**, **Device Manager** tab. Open the **CD-ROM** folder then click the name which corresponds to your active CD-ROM drive and click the **Settings** tab).

➤ **To change the volume**, go to the **Volume Control** panel by using **View - Volume Control**.

The application window appears.

In the **CD Audio** section, slide the **Balance** cursor to define the sound balance between the two speakers. In **Volume**, slide the cursor up to increase the volume, or down to decrease.

The *Mute* option cuts off the sound.

You can then minimize the **Volume Control** window or close it if you have finished using it.

126                                                         Windows 98

# CD Player

## Listening to an audio CD

*The **Total Play** information (bottom left) tells you the precise length in time of your CD.*

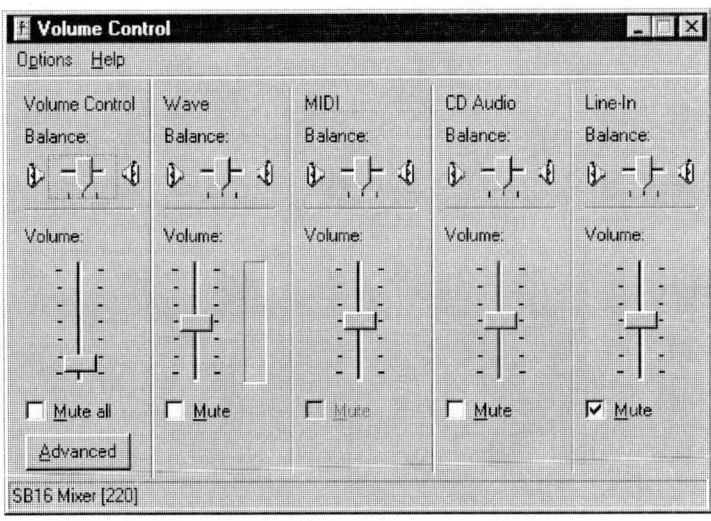

*Using **Options - Properties** here, you can change the number of volume controls being displayed.*

Windows 98     127

MULTIMEDIA

## Naming and selecting tracks on an audio CD

While in the **CD Player** application, choose:

**Disc - Edit Play List**

> In **Available Tracks**, click the track you wish to name, then select the generic name which appears in the **Track (no.)** text box. Now type in the title corresponding to the track before clicking **Set Name**. Proceed in the same way for all the tracks on the CD.
>
> **To select a track to play**, click the **Clear All** button to empty the **Play List**, then click the first track you want to select. Add to the **Play List** by clicking **Add**; proceed in the same way for each track that you want to play.
>
> Use these buttons:
>
> Remove     to remove one of the titles from the list.
> Reset        to reinsert every track onto the **Play List**.
>
> Click **OK** then start playing the CD as required.

## Playing a multimedia file

Once in the **Media Player** application, use the **Device** menu to choose a device depending on what type of file you wish to play.

*The list of devices can vary largely between computers, depending on their software and hardware. You should however systematically find **Video for Windows** which will open the application that manages AVI and **Active Movie** format files.*

Open, if necessary, the multimedia file you want to play. This is not necessary in the case of an audio CD.

> Click the ▶ button to play the multimedia file.
>
> *The first track will be played. While you cannot select the particular tracks you want to play, you can move on to the next track.*
>
> *The Media player can play audio CDs as well as moving image files.*

Windows 98

## CD Player

### Naming and selecting tracks on an audio CD

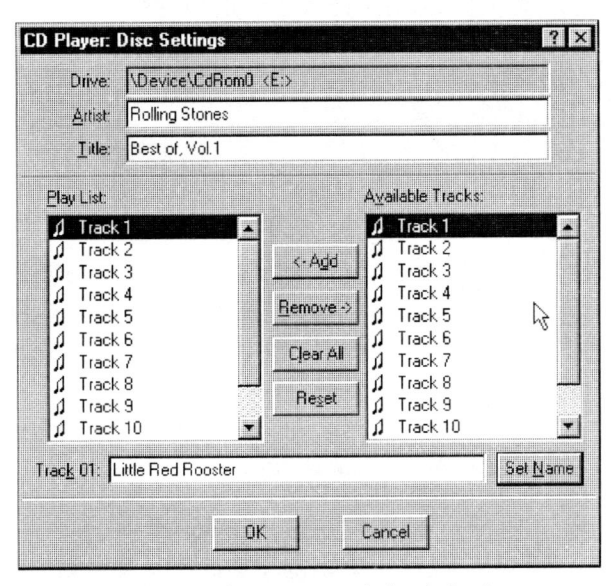

*You can also use the top part of the dialog box to note the name of the artist and the title of the CD.*

### Playing a multimedia file

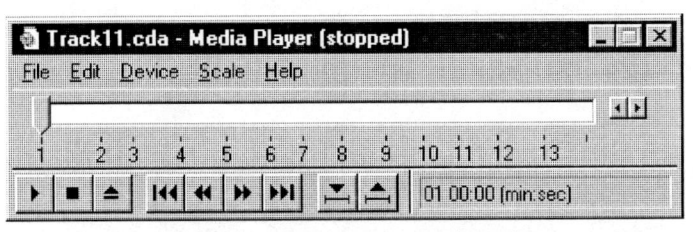

*The track numbers appear in the window: the interval between each number is proportional to the length of the track.*

Windows 98

129

MULTIMEDIA

## Copying part of a multimedia file

To select part of the file, click the ▼ button when the cursor reaches the beginning of the section you wish to select.

☞ Let the track(s) play, then click ▲ when the cursor reaches the end of the section you want to select.

To play only the chosen section, press [Alt] **P**.

*Once the item has finished, playing will stop automatically.*

To copy the selected part onto the clipboard, use **Edit - Copy Object** or [Ctrl] **C**.

Access the destination application, go to the place where you wish to insert the item and use **Edit - Paste** to paste the information.

*You can reduce the size of the pasted object by dragging one of its handles.*

☞ Double-click the picture to run the multimedia file.

*If the **Control Bar on Playback** option is active in the **Media Player** application (**Edit - Options**), a control bar under the picture indicates how much of the file has been played.*

**To view a video with a different screen size**, open the .AVI video file concerned.

**Device - Properties**

Choose a **Window size** using the corresponding drop-down list (**Double original size, 1/16 of screen size...**)

or

click **Full Screen**.

Click **OK**.

130                                                                                               Windows 98

# Media Player

## Copying part of a multimedia file

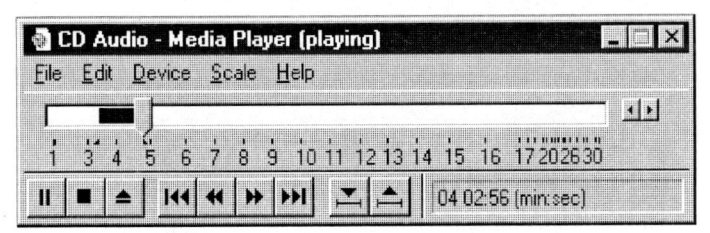

*The selected item is represented on the screen by two triangles and a blue band.*

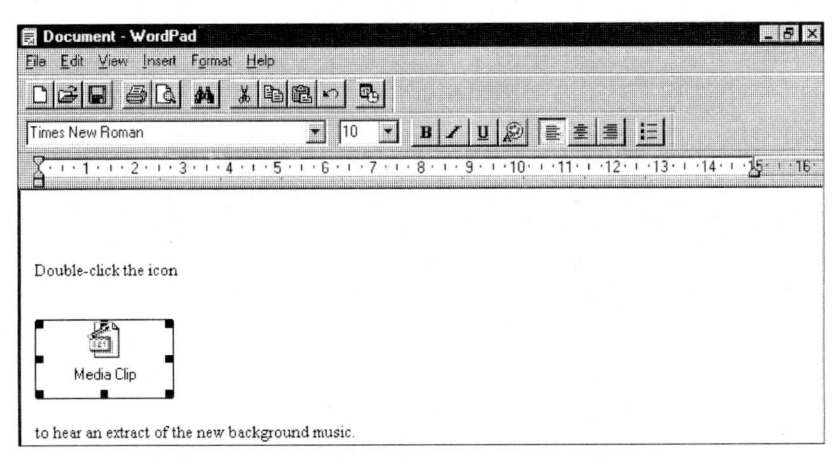

*Selection handles appear when the object is selected.*

MULTIMEDIA

## Playing a sound file (Sound Recorder)

Go into the **Sound Recorder** multimedia application.

Open the .WAV sound document that you want to listen to using **File - Open**.

> Click the ▶ button to play.

*You can adjust the volume by going into the Volume Control application or by using the corresponding options in the Effects menu.*

*You will also find in this menu commands for changing the playing speed, adding echo, reversing playing order...*

> **To extract part of a sound file**, play the sound file and click the ■ button at the beginning of the part you want to extract.

Use the **Edit - Delete before current position** command and click **OK** to confirm.

Continue playing the file and click ■ when the end of the required part is reached.

Use the **Edit - Delete after current position** command and confirm by clicking **OK**.

Now, choose **File - Save As** to save the shortened file under a different name.

**To copy a sound document into another document**, use the **Edit - Copy** command or `Ctrl` **C**.

*The document is transferred to the Windows clipboard and you can embed it into a document from another application, such as WordPad.*

Open the destination document.

Access the place where you wish to insert the sound item and use **Edit - Paste Insert** or `Ctrl` **V**.

> To retrieve the sound file as it exists on the disk, use the **File - Revert** command and click **Yes** to confirm.

# Sound Recorder

## Playing a sound file (Sound Recorder)

*The sound wavelength appears in the window.*

*The position is specified in seconds.*

Windows 98

133

# MULTIMEDIA

## Recording with a microphone

*If you have a microphone, the Sound Recorder application makes it possible to record your own voice. You can for example, make files containing comments that can be inserted into applications.*

**To record your voice with the microphone**, create a new document using **File - New**.

To choose the correct recording quality, use **File - Properties** then click **Convert Now**. Select the required quality from the **Name** list.

*The higher the quality, the shorter the recording time available and the more voluminous the files created. The best quality is produced by using the parameters entitled **CD Quality**.*

Ensure that the microphone is correctly plugged in then click [●].

Speak your text into the microphone then click [■] to stop recording.

Save your document.

*If an audio CD is being played at the same time as you are using the microphone, the music will be recorded as background music to your commentaries.*

**To record from an audio CD**, create a new document in the **Sound Recorder** application.

➪ Choose a superior recording quality: **File - Properties - Convert Now**, and choose **CD Quality** in the **Name** list and confirm.

Start playing the audio CD from the **CD Player**.

Minimize this application window if you like then click [●] to start recording.

*There is a limited recording time allowed.*

To stop recording, click the [■] button on the **Sound Recorder**, then go into the CD Player window to stop the CD.

Go back into **Sound Recorder** and if required, save the extract.

# Sound Recorder

## Recording with a microphone

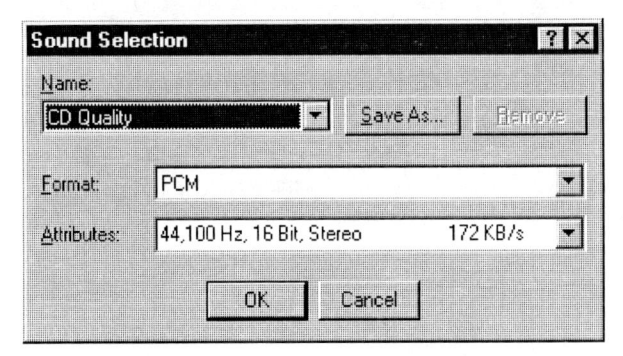

*The best sound quality is produced by the **CD Quality** group of parameters.*

MULTIMEDIA

## Modifying sound files

**To mix two sound files**, open one of the sound documents and go to the point where you wish to mix in the other.

**Edit - Mix with File**

> Double-click the sound document you want to mix in.

*This allows you to mix together the two sound files (for example, an audio CD and a voice recording).*

*Play it through to check.*

*Words and music can now be heard together in the same document.*

Remember that you can obtain a similar effect by playing an audio CD while you record your voice.

*You can also copy the extract to be mixed into the clipboard then paste it into the destination document, using* **Edit - Paste Mix**.

**To increase recording time**, after having created a new document, make a blank recording; click [●] and let the slider run the required time without recording any sound.

Next copy this blank piece of recording using **Edit - Copy**.

Create a new document (do not save the first one).

Click [●] and let the slider run to the end.

Then use **Edit - Paste Insert** to paste in the blank recording time previously copied in the clipboard.

*You now have double the previous recording time at your disposition.*

Click [◄◄] then make your recording or click [►►] to go to the end of the file if you wish to paste in more recording time from the clipboard.

*Be careful: after a certain recording time is reached, the created sound documents quickly become very large.*

136  Windows 98

# Sound Recorder

## Modifying sound files

# MULTIMEDIA

## YOUR NOTES

# Chapter 6

## OLE/CONFIGURATION

- **OBJECT LINKING AND EMBEDDING**  p.140
- **CONFIGURATION**  p.148

## OLE/CONFIGURATION

## Inserting an existing document into another document

By using the technique of Object Linking and Embedding (also known as **OLE**), Windows optimises the transfer of data between applications. Data can be inserted into a document from another application in one of two ways:
- using **embedding**, the embedded object becomes an integral part of the destination document (the size of the document increases in consequence).
- using **linking**, the destination document does not contain the transferred object: it contains a linking formula indicating where the object can be found when the application needs it (to display or to print).

Here are definitions of three terms you will see frequently in the next few pages:
- an **object** is any item you can create from an application (it may be a table or a chart from a spreadsheet, artwork from a drawing application, sound or an image from a multimedia application...),
- only **server** applications can produce objects which may be inserted into other applications (for example, Paint, Sound Recorder, the spread sheet Excel...),
- only **client** applications can accept the insertion of an object (this is the case with WordPad or the word processor Word for Windows...). Some applications can be both clients and servers.

**To insert an existing document**, open the destination document from the client application (for example WordPad), then access the place where you wish to insert the document.

**Insert - Object...**

This command can vary slightly form one application to the next.

Activate the **Create from File** option.

> Give the document name in the **File** text box or click the **Browse** button to find it in the file hierarchy.
>
> The name of the document is preceded by its path.
>
> Activate the **Link** option if the object is to be linked and not embedded.
>
> Activate **Display as Icon** if you want an icon to represent the source file in the client application.
>
> Click **OK**.
>
> Double-click the inserted document to start the server application.

140

Windows 98

# Object linking and embedding

## Inserting an existing document into another document

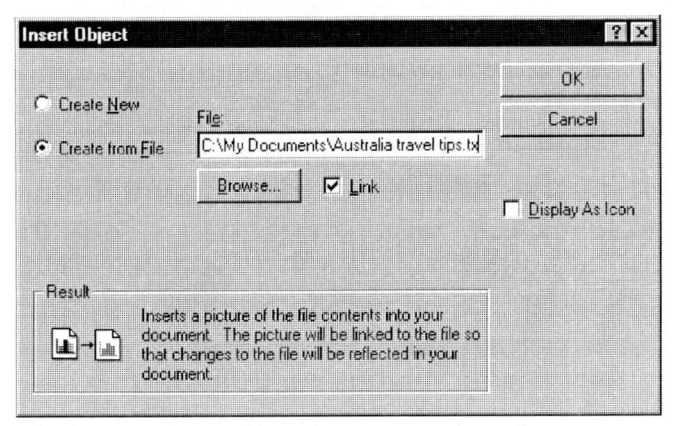

*An object can be a table, a chart, a picture, sound or an image.*

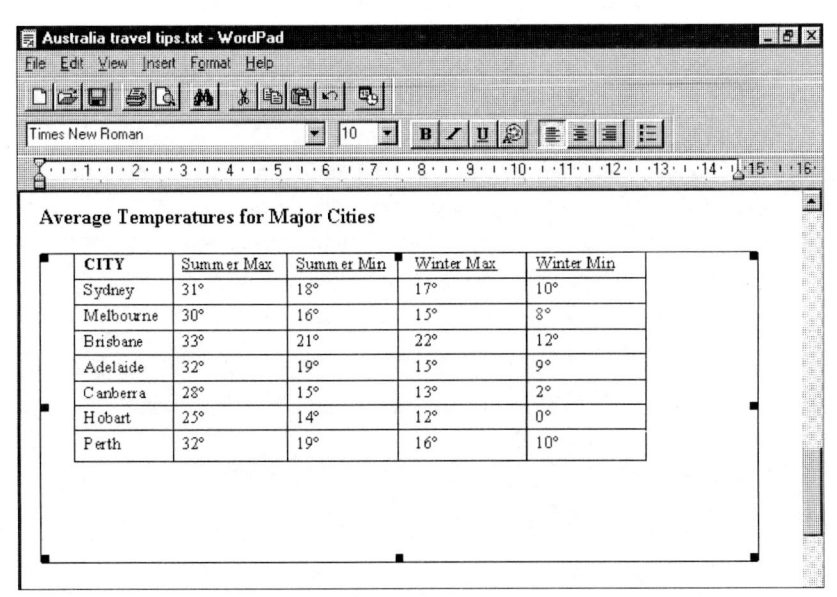

*The inserted item from the server application appears; the selected object has selection handles.*

Windows 98

141

# OLE/CONFIGURATION

## Inserting a new document into another document

From the client application, access the place where you want to insert the object.

**Insert - Object...**

> Activate the **Create New** option then select the type of object depending on which application you want to run to create it.

Activate **Display as Icon** if you want the object to be represented as an icon in the destination document.

Click **OK**.

*The server application window replaces the client application window. This is "in-place" editing: the client application document is still visible but the client application window is temporarily replaced to allow you to create your object. This technique is only available for certain applications; for others, the server application appears in a distinct window which is placed over that of the client application.*

*The document you are going to create in the server application will be embedded in the client application document. You will not be able to open, nor modify it without first opening the client application document.*

> Create the object using the tools and options of the server application.

To find the client application again, proceed in this way:
- if the server application appears in a distinct window, close this window and click **Yes** to update the document in the client application.
- if using in-place editing, click anywhere else in the window outside the inserted object.

*You will find yourself back in the client application window and document.*

# Object linking and embedding

## Inserting a new document into another document

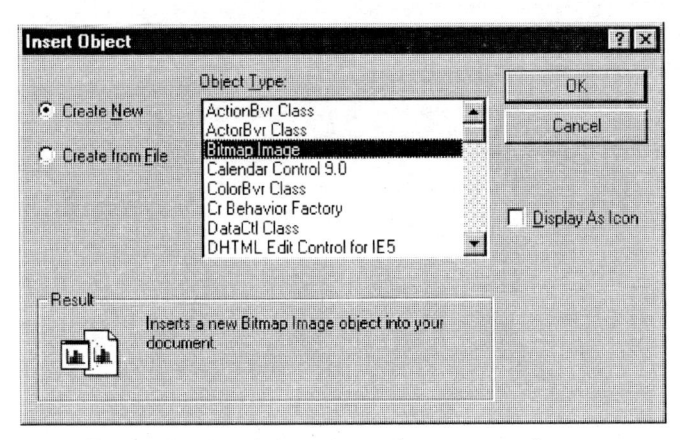

*The list displayed depends on the server applications installed on your disk.*

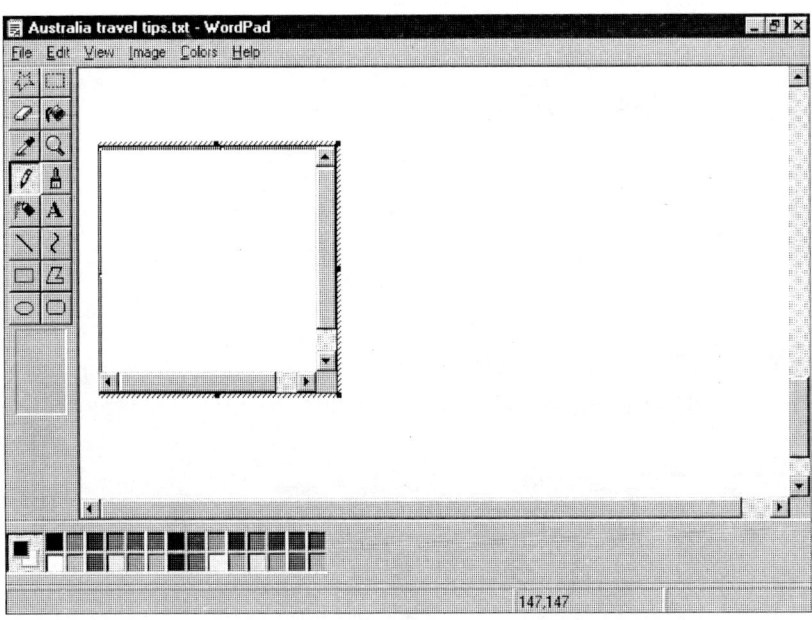

*The **Paint** menus and toolbox appear in the **WordPad** window.*

Windows 98

143

# OLE/CONFIGURATION

## Managing a link with an external object

When you insert an object by making a link, the destination document contains a reference corresponding to the source document. By default, the object is automatically updated.

From the destination document, use the **Edit - Links** command.
You will see the list of documents linked with the active document.

> Select the link you wish to work with by clicking the corresponding line in the list.
> 
> Define the type of update, either **Automatic** or **Manual**.
> 
> If you have chosen **Manual** update, click the **Update Now** button to update the object in the destination document.
> 
> The *Open Source* button opens the source document to allow any changes required. The *Change Source* button can be used if the source document has been moved.
> 
> Click either **Cancel** or **OK** to close the dialogue box.

## Modifying an embedded object

To edit the embedded object in place, double-click the inserted object or use **Edit - ...Object - Edit**. To open the server application in a new window, use **Edit - ...Object - Open**.

*...* represents the type of object inserted, for example Bitmap Image Object, Wave Sound Object...

As it did when the object was created, the server application window temporarily replaces the client application window; you can see by its title that the image you are working on belongs to the client application.

> Make the desired changes.
> 
> Close the server application window, or if editing in place, click elsewhere in the document to activate the client application.

# Object linking and embedding

## Managing a link with an external object

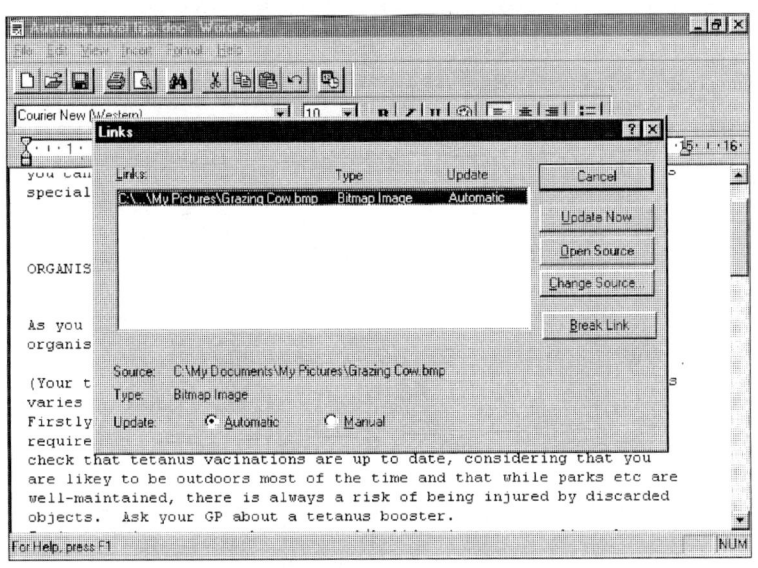

*The WordPad document contains an automatic link with the **Island.bmp** document. If this was to be modified, the contents of the WordPad document would be automatically updated.*

## Modifying an embedded object

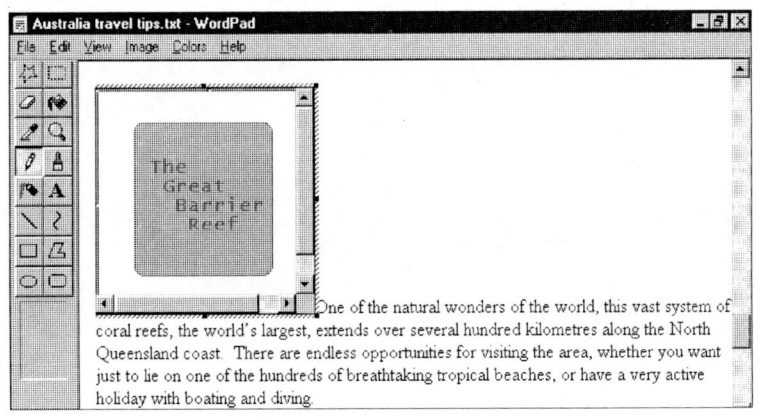

*The title **The Great Barrier Reef** has been created in Paint and embedded into WordPad.*

OLE / CONFIGURATION

## Displaying an embedded object as an icon

Click the object to select it then choose **Edit - Object Properties** or [Alt][Enter].
You can also right-click the object and choose *Object Properties*.

Click the **View** tab.

Activate the **Display as Icon** option.

Click **Change Icon** if you are not satisfied with the icon proposed.

> Select the desired icon or click **Browse** to select an icon from another application.
>
> The *Default* option chooses the icon corresponding to the source application.
>
> Use the **Label** text box to enter a text to appear under the icon.
>
> Click **OK**.
>
> The *Apply* button in the *Properties* dialog box lets you apply the changes specified in the dialog box without closing it.
>
> Click **OK** to close the **Properties** dialog box.
>
> To display an object's contents, double-click its icon.

# Object linking and embedding

## Displaying an embedded object as an icon

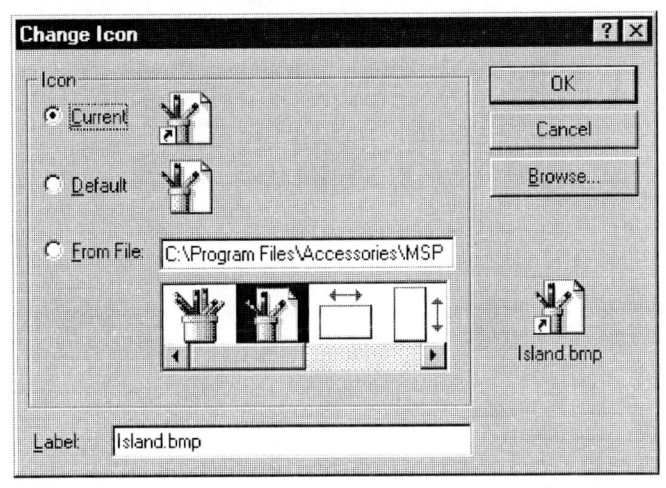

*You can personalise the icon by entering a particular name in the **Label** box.*

OLE / CONFIGURATION

## Clearing the Documents menu

*The Documents menu contains the names of the last fifteen files used.*

Right-click the task bar and choose **Properties** or use **Start - Parameters - Taskbar and Start Menu.**

> In the **Start Menu Programs** page, click **Clear.**
> Click **OK**.

## Creating a shortcut on the Desktop

*A shortcut represents an object such as a document, an application or a drive. It can be inserted onto the Desktop so that the document is immediately accessible when you access Windows.*

Start the Explorer, but do not maximize the window: make sure a part of the desktop is visible in the background.

> Drag the document, application or folder icon onto the Desktop.
>
> *Windows 98 automatically creates a shortcut to the document, folder or application.*
>
> *If you drag the icon of the floppy disk drive, Windows 98 will offer to create a shortcut. Click Yes to confirm creating the shortcut.*
>
> To start the application corresponding to the shortcut, or to open a document or folder, double-click the shortcut icon.

# Configuration

## Clearing the Documents menu

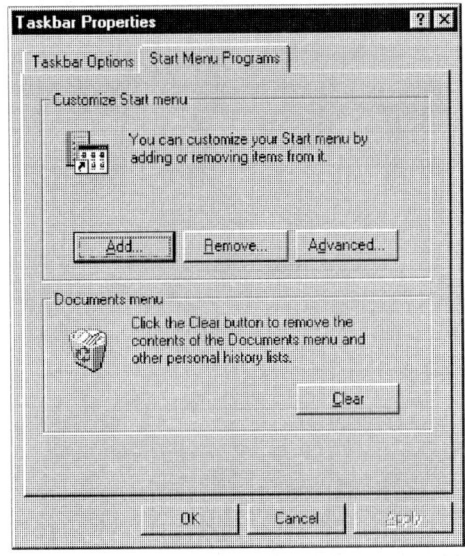

*A partial clearing of the Documents menu is not possible.*

## Creating a shortcut on the Desktop

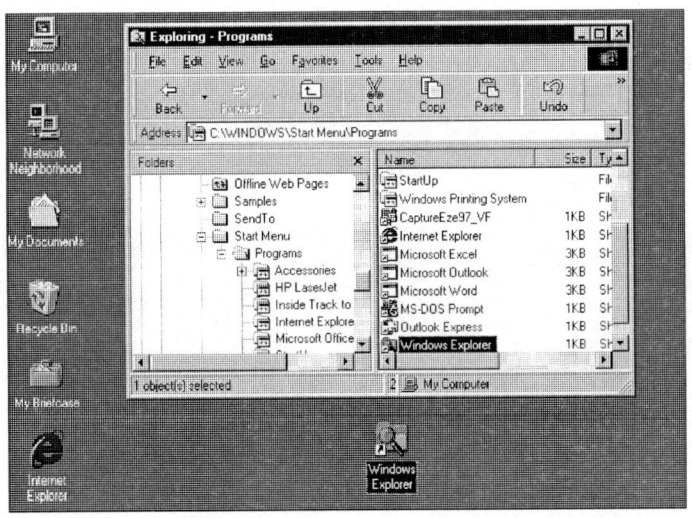

*Notice that a shortcut icon is accompanied by a small arrow.*

Windows 98

OLE / CONFIGURATION

## Presenting the Desktop

**To change the presentation of the Desktop**, right-click an empty space on the Desktop and choose **Properties**.

> On the **Background** page, choose the design which will appear as the background, or wallpaper, for the Desktop.
>
> Specify how the design will be displayed using the **Display** list:
>
> Center        the image appears in the centre of the screen.
> Tile          the image is repeated all over the Desktop.
> Stretch       the image is enlarged to fill the whole Desktop area.
>
> The *Apply* button lets you apply the wallpaper without closing the dialog box.
>
> You can also change one of the patterns by using the *Browse* button to access the file hierarchy and choose a file (for example with extension BMP, GIF or JPEG) containing a graphic image which can be used as wallpaper.
>
> You can also apply wallpaper from the Paint application.

> **To install a screen saver**, select one from the list on the **Screen Saver** page. Specify how long the computer should be inactive before the screen saver appears in the **Wait** box.
>
> You will see the chosen screen saver in the small screen.
>
> The *Preview* button lets you see the screen saver on the full screen (move the mouse to return to the dialog box).
>
> Click the **Settings** button to define the parameters for the chosen screen saver (for example, if you choose the **Scrolling Marquee** screen saver, you can specify the text which will displayed on the screen saver screen).

# Configuration

## Presenting the Desktop

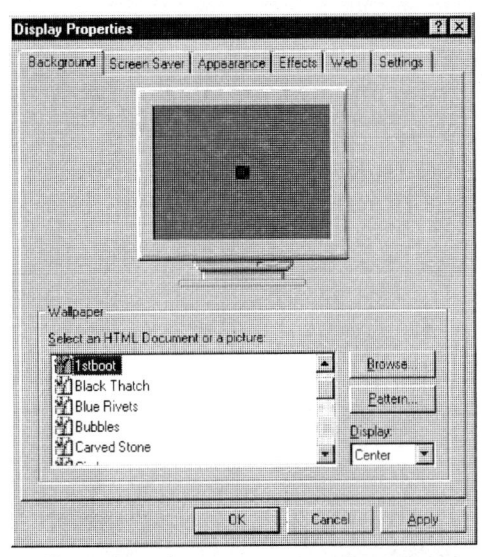

*The selected parameters can be seen in the sample screen displayed in the dialog box.*

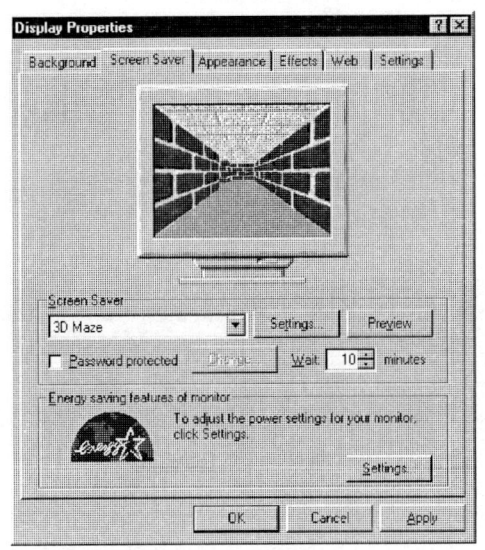

*The normal inactivity time for a workstation is 60 minutes.*

Windows 98

# OLE/CONFIGURATION

## Modifying the control date and time

Double-click the time displayed on the taskbar or start the **Date/Time** application located in the Control Panel.

> Specify the required date and time using the corresponding lists or text boxes.
>
> The *Time Zone* page allows you to select the time zone corresponding to your country and to automatically adjust to any seasonal time changes (summer time...).
>
> Click **OK**.

## Managing the taskbar

**To move the taskbar**, drag it to another side of the screen.

**To change its height, or width**, point to its upper side (or left side) and drag to size.

**To define the toolbars to be displayed on the taskbar**, right-click the taskbar, point to the **Toolbars** option to see the list containing the toolbars that can be shown. Activate the ones to show; deactivate the ones to hide.

**To move one of the toolbars on the taskbar**, drag the vertical handle situated to the left of the bar.

**To hide the taskbar**, right-click an empty space on the bar then choose **Properties**:

> Activate one of these options:
>
> Always on top   so that the bar stays on the screen even when the active application is displayed full screen.
>
> Auto hide   so that the taskbar is minimized to a line at the bottom of the screen. If you point to the line, the taskbar will appear and you can use it as usual.

# Configuration

## Modifying the control date and time

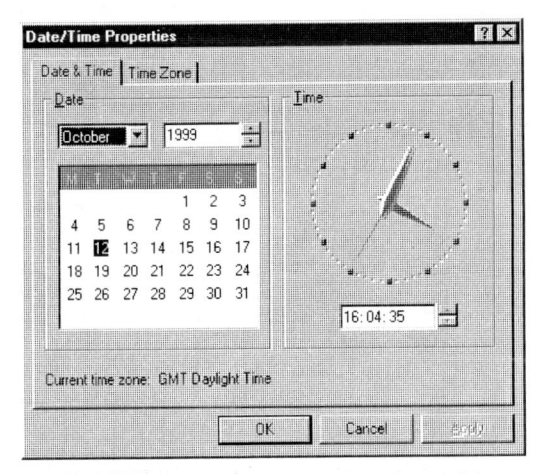

*By default, Windows automatically changes the time when summer time or winter time are introduced.*

## Managing the taskbar

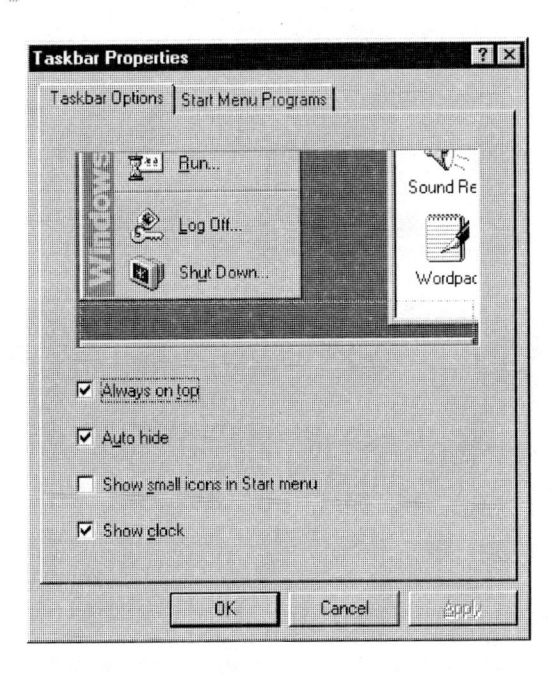

OLE / CONFIGURATION

## Installing a printer

Open the **Printers** folder situated in the Control Panel.

Double-click the **Add Printer** icon.

*Windows 98 starts the corresponding Wizard.*

Click the **Next** button.

> Indicate whether you are installing a **Local printer** or a **Network printer** then click **Next**.
>
> If you are installing a network printer, give the network path to the printer then click **Next**.
>
> Specify the name of the printer then click **Next**.
>
> If you are installing a local printer, specify the communication port.
>
> Indicate whether Windows applications work with this printer by default, then click **Next**.
>
> Indicate if you want to print a test page, then click **Finish**.
>
> Insert the CD ROM containing the programme, or the floppy disk that Windows asks for, and click **OK**.

# Configuration

## Installing a printer

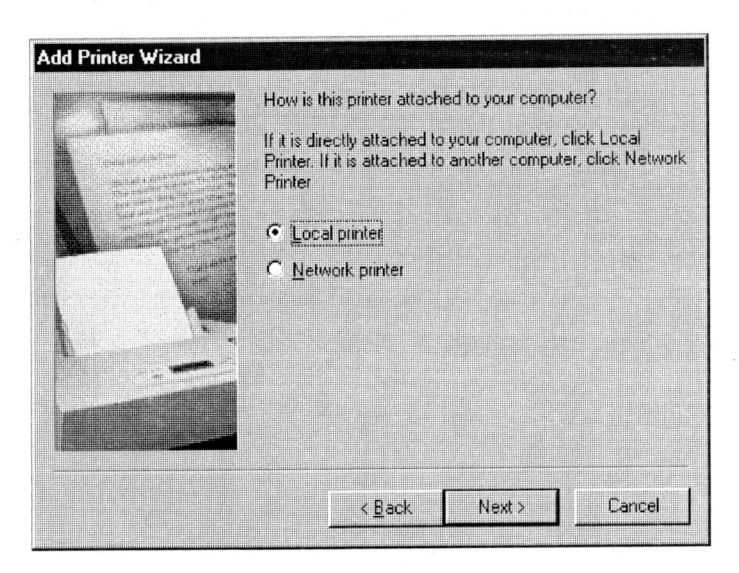

**Add Printer Wizard**

How is this printer attached to your computer?

If it is directly attached to your computer, click Local Printer. If it is attached to another computer, click Network Printer

- ⦿ Local printer
- ○ Network printer

[< Back] [Next >] [Cancel]

Windows 98

# OLE/CONFIGURATION

## YOUR NOTES

# Shortcut keys

## Operating system shortcut keys

| | |
|---|---|
| [F1] | Display the **Help Topics** dialog box. |
| [Alt][F4] | Leave an application. |
| [Shift][F10] | Display a selection shortcut menu. |
| [Ctrl] X | Cut the selection. |
| [Ctrl] C | Copy the selection. |
| [Ctrl] V | Paste the selection. |
| [Del] | Delete a folder or document. |
| [Ctrl] Z | Undo the last action. |
| [Ctrl][Esc] | Open the **Start** menu. |
| [Alt][⇄] | Activate an application which is already open. |

## Desktop and Windows Explorer

| | |
|---|---|
| [F2] | Rename a folder or document. |
| [F3] | Display the **Find** dialog box. |
| [Shift][Del] | Delete a file without sending it to the Recycle bin. |
| [Alt][Enter] | Display the selected object's properties. |

## My Computer and the Explorer

| | |
|---|---|
| [F5] | Refresh the window. |
| [Ctrl] G | Go to. |
| [Ctrl] A | Select all. |
| [←] | Display the folder above, if a folder has been selected. |

## Explorer only

| | |
|---|---|
| [F6] | Go from one pane to another. |
| * | Expand branch completely (folders and sub-folders). |
| + | Expand a branch. |
| - | Collapse a branch. |
| [→] | Expand branch, or, if it is already expanded, select the first sub-folder. |
| [←] | Collapse branch, or, if it is already collapsed, select the folder above. |

Windows 98

157

# APPENDIX

## Properties dialog box

`Ctrl` `Tab`　　　　　　Activate the next page.
`Ctrl` `Shift` `Tab`　　　Activate the previous page.

## Open and Save As dialog box

`F4`　　　　　　Open the **Look in** list.
`F5`　　　　　　Refresh the dialog box.
`←`　　　　　　If you have selected a folder open the parent folder.

# INDEX

## !

| | |
|---|---|
| Control date and time | 152 |
| Dialog boxes | 22 |
| Managing Windows | 16 |
| Menus | 20 |
| Shutting down | 14 |
| Starting Windows 98 | 8 |
| Taskbar | 152 |
| Undoing an action | 26 |
| Working in dialog boxes | 22 |

## A

### ACCESSORIES

| | |
|---|---|
| Multimedia | 126 |
| Paint | 68 |
| WordPad | 38 |

### APPLICATIONS

| | |
|---|---|
| Creating documents | 32 |
| Leaving | 14 |
| Managing menus | 20 |
| Opening (Start menu) | 14 |
| Opening document | 30 |
| Opening applications with Explorer | 118 |

See also ACCESSORIES

## C

### CD PLAYER

| | |
|---|---|
| Listening to an audio CD | 126 |
| Managing CD tracks | 128 |

See also MULTIMEDIA

### CHARACTERS

| | |
|---|---|
| Applying attributes to characters | 48 - 49 |
| Applying attributes (WordPad) | 48 |
| Changing attributes (WordPad) | 52 |
| Changing the font | 49 |
| Changing the font size | 50 - 51 |
| Changing the indents | 52 |
| Colouring characters | 50 - 51 |
| Colouring (WordPad) | 50 |

See also TEXT

### CLIPBOARD

| | |
|---|---|
| Copying folders or documents (Explorer) | 112 |
| Copying/moving text (WordPad) | 46 |
| Moving folders or documents (Explorer) | 116 |

### COLOURS

| | |
|---|---|
| Customising (Paint) | 86 |
| Filling an area (Paint) | 86 |
| Managing (Paint) | 88 |

See also PAINT

### CONFIGURATION

| | |
|---|---|
| Changing the date and time | 152 |
| Inserting a document into another | 140 |
| Inserting a new document into an existing one | 142 |
| Installing a printer | 154 |
| Managing the Task bar | 152 |

### COPYING

| | |
|---|---|
| Copying an image inside the image area (Paint | 82 |
| Copying folders or documents (Explorer) | 112 |
| Copying folders or documents to a diskette | 114 |
| Copying part of a multimedia file | 130 |
| Copying the contents of a document (Paint) | 84 |
| Copying to a new document (Paint) | 84 |
| Copying/moving text with the Clipboard (WordPad) | 46 |

Windows 98

# INDEX

## D

### DATE
| | |
|---|---|
| Changing the control date | 152 |
| Inserting the date into a document (WordPad) | 42 |

### DESKTOP
| | |
|---|---|
| Contents | 10 |
| Creating shortcuts | 148 |
| Presentation | 150 |
| Wallpapering (Paint) | 88 |

### DISKETTE
| | |
|---|---|
| Copying folders or documents to a diskette | 114 |

### DOCUMENTS
| | |
|---|---|
| Clearing the Documents menu | 148 |
| Copying to a diskette (Explorer) | 114 |
| Creating | 32 |
| Finding with Explorer | 108, 110 |
| Inserting | 142 |
| Insertion (WordPad) | 140 |
| Managing in Explorer | 112 |
| Opening from Start menu | 32 |
| Opening in an application | 30 |
| Printing (Explorer) | 120 |
| Saving | 34 |
| Selecting/deselecting in Explorer | 106 |

*See also OLE, PRINTING*

### DRAWING
| | |
|---|---|
| Drawing a rectangle, square, circle or ellips (Pai | 72 |
| Drawing a straight or curved line | 74 |
| Drawing a triangle or polygon | 76 |

*See also PAINT, IMAGES*

### DRIVES
| | |
|---|---|
| Accessing (without Explorer) | 26 |
| Accessing from Explorer | 102 |

## E

### EXPLORER
| | |
|---|---|
| Accessing drives/folders | 102 |
| Application (opening) | 118 |
| Creating folders | 110 |
| Finding documents | 108, 110 |
| Managing folders and documents | 112 |
| Managing the view | 104 |
| Moving folders or documents | 116 |
| Printing documents | 120 |
| Selecting/deselecting documents | 106 |
| Sharing | 122 |
| The Recycle Bin | 120 |
| Window | 98 |

## F

### FINDING
| | |
|---|---|
| Finding documents by date | 110 |
| Finding documents by name | 108 |
| Finding text (WordPad) | 44 |
| Finding/replacing text (WordPad) | 46 |
| Moving an image (Paint) | 80 |
| Moving folders or documents | 116 |

*See also COPYING*

### FOLDERS
| | |
|---|---|
| Accessing shared folders without Explorer | 28 |
| Accessing with Explorer | 102 |
| Copying to a diskette (Explorer) | 114 |
| Creating (Explorer) | 110 |
| Managing in Explorer | 112 |
| Sharing (Explorer) | 122 |

### FORMATTING
| | |
|---|---|
| Indents (WordPad) | 52 |
| Inserting bullets (WordPad) | 56 |
| Paragraph indents (WordPad) | 52 |

# INDEX

Tabs (WordPad) 56, 58
Text alignment (WordPad) 54

*See also* PARAGRAPHS

## H

### HELP

Windows Help menu 24

## I

### IMAGES

Creation (Paint) 70
Erasing (Paint) 80
Moving (Paint) 80
Polygons (Paint) 76
Rectangles, squares, circles,
ellipsis (Paint 72
Resizing, skewing, rotating (Paint) 92
Selecting copying (Paint) 82

*See also* PAINT

### INSTALLATION

Printers 154

## L

### LINKING

*See* OLE

## M

### MOVING

Moving the insertion point
in WordPad 40

### MULTIMEDIA

CD Player 126
Listening to an audio CD 126
Managing the CD tracks 128
Modifying sound files 136
Playing a multimedia file
(Media Player) 128
Recording with a microphone 134
Sound Recorder 132

## N

### NETWORKS

Sharing folders with other users
(Explorer) 122

## O

### OLE

Displaying an embedded object
as an icon 146
Embedded object (editing) 144
Inserting (documents) 140
Link (Managing) 144

## P

### PAINT

Colours (filling anarea) 86
Colours (managing) 86, 88
Image (creating) 70
Image (resizing, skewing, rotating) 94
Images (erasing) 80
Images (moving) 80
Images (resizing, skewing, rotating) 92
Paint application 68
Zoom 90

*See also* IMAGES

Windows 98 161

# INDEX

## PARAGRAPHS

| | |
|---|---|
| Formatting (WordPad) | 54 |
| Inserting bullets (WordPad) | 56 |
| Tabs (WordPad) | 58 |
| Text alignment (WordPad) | 54 |

See also FORMATTING

## PREVIEW

| | |
|---|---|
| Print preview in WordPad | 60 |

## PRINTING

| | |
|---|---|
| Installing a printer (Control Panel) | 154 |
| Page setup (WordPad) | 60 |
| Print preview (WordPad) | 60 |
| Print Queue (managing) | 64 |
| Printing from Explorer | 120 |
| WordPad documents | 62 |

## S

### SELECTING

| | |
|---|---|
| Selecting part of an image (Paint) | 82 |
| Selecting text (WordPad) | 40 |
| Selecting/deselecting documents (Explorer) | 106 |

### SHORTCUTS

| | |
|---|---|
| Creating | 148 |

### SOUND FILES

| | |
|---|---|
| Modifying | 136 |

### SOUND RECORDER

| | |
|---|---|
| Recording with a microphe | 134 |
| Sound recorder | 132 |

### SOUNDFILES

See MULTIMEDIA

## START MENU

| | |
|---|---|
| Clearing the Documents menu | 148 |
| Description | 12 |
| Documents menu (opening) | 32 |
| Starting an application | 14 |

## T

### TASKBAR

| | |
|---|---|
| Managing | 152 |

### TEXT

| | |
|---|---|
| Applying attributes to characters (WordPad) | 48 |
| Changing (WordPad) | 48, 50 |
| Changing the alignment (WordPad) | 54 |
| Copying/moving (WordPad) | 46 |
| Entering/changing (WordPad) | 42 |
| Finding (WordPad) | 44 |
| Managing text in Paint | 78 |
| Replacing (WordPad) | 46 |
| Selecting (WordPad) | 40 |

See also CHARACTERS

## W

### WINDOWS

| | |
|---|---|
| Managing one Window | 16 |
| Managing several Windows | 18 |

See also individual applications

## Z

### ZOOM

| | |
|---|---|
| Using zoom (Paint) | 90 |